OUT
HOME

A Bur Oak Book

John Madson

OUT HOME

edited by Michael McIntosh

illustrations by Dycie Madson

UNIVERSITY OF IOWA PRESS
IOWA CITY

University of Iowa Press, Iowa City 52242
www.uiowapress.org
Copyright © 1979 by John Madson and Michael McIntosh
Originally published by Winchester Press
First University of Iowa Press edition, 2008
Printed in the United States of America

The University of Iowa Press is a member of Green Press
Initiative and is committed to preserving natural resources.

Printed on acid-free paper

Library of Congress Cataloging-in-Publication Data
Madson, John.
    Out home / by John Madson; edited by Michael
McIntosh; illustrations by Dycie Madson.—1st University
of Iowa Press ed.
        p.   cm.
    Originally published: John Madson, out home.
    New York: Winchester Press, c1979.
    ISBN-13: 978-1-58729-688-8 (pbk.)
    ISBN-10: 1-58729-688-8 (pbk.)
    1. Nature. 2. Outdoor life. I. McIntosh, Michael. II. Title.
    QH81.M2 2008   2008004166
    799.2—dc22

08 09 10 11 12 P 5 4 3 2 1

Contents

Introduction to the Second Coming of *Out Home*   vii

Introduction   ix

Part I 〜 Out Home

   Going Out More   3
   An Outdoor Ledger   11
   Dallas Morgan and the Lion   15
   Palace in the Popple   31
   The Secret Life of the Cottontail Deer   33
   The Bum Husband   41
   The Passing of Little Sam   43
   Pheasants Beyond Autumn   45

Part II 〜 Under the Sun, by the Side of the Wind

   Message from a Desert Island   57
   Requiem for a Small River   67
   The Running Country   73
   The Prairie Blizzard   93
   Where the River Fits the Song   103
   The High Beyond   123

Part III ᪥ Old Friends

Giants in the Cliffs   127
The Dance on Monkey Mountain   139
Day of the Crane   155
North Again   159

Part IV ᪥ The Horizons of Home

A Letter to a Young Trapper   179
Poor Cousins   185
The Dragons Are Bigger Today   191
Something for the Kids   199

Introduction to the
Second Coming of *Out Home*

Sometimes it seems as if the farther we go, the closer we are to where we started.

Out Home was my first book. That was twenty-six books ago. And after forty years of living in other states, I find myself back in Iowa, less than an hour from where I was born and about an hour and a half from where John was born. The landscape is different from what we once knew, but the good parts are still here.

I don't know what to say about John Madson that I haven't already said. He was my hero as a writer and still is. He was a consummate storyteller who could have you in stitches or tears and sometimes both at once. We were close friends for the last twenty years of his life, and I miss him. I could tell you endless stories about the time we spent together in Arkansas and Missouri and Montana and some other places—but better you hear them from him.

For now, I will simply offer thanks to John's wife, Dycie, for her help and unending support. And to Holly Carver of the University of Iowa Press for her appreciation of the finest voice that ever spoke of the wonders to be found out home.

Michael McIntosh, The Cornfields, Marion County, Iowa, 2008

Introduction

This book began, as many good things do, in the spring. And it began out home—deep in the Ouachita Mountains of Arkansas, in a turkey camp on a pine ridge just shouting distance from Muddy Creek.

It was the introspective hour. The sun was disappearing out over Oklahoma and the last roosting turkey had gobbled somewhere off to the east. There wasn't much talk in camp; most of us were making a slow transition from the silence of a day's turkey hunting to the time, later, when the hissing Colemans would light up our ridgetop with their thin, greenish glare, when we would ease back into the chatter of tired hunters glad to be together again.

John and I were sitting by the fire, indulging our mutual fondness for thick Louisiana coffee and talking haphazardly about two other loves we share—the outdoors and its literature. Somewhere along the way, a familiar thought occurred to me— it's impossible to talk about the best outdoor literature of the mid-twentieth century without talking about John Madson.

So I did. I talked about his story on the Delta Marsh that had come out the month before in *Audubon*, and he went on to tell me about a bee-tree piece that was in the mill for fall. My memory began sifting back through the magazine pieces John has written over the past few years, and I thought once again that they were just too good to be left lying piecemeal in the gloom of the bound periodicals section. I'm afraid I lost the thread of the bee-tree story about then, because a book was beginning to take shape in my mind—a book of wonderful stories about the earth and its creatures, a book by the man who, better than any writer today, captures the fine, bright love of the outdoors in prose as good as prose can be.

It would be nice if books could be completed as simply and effortlessly as they are sometimes conceived. But, of course, it cannot be so. Since that spring night in the Ouachitas when I sat musing between the wild turkeys and the sunset, there have been months of work, months of reading and re-reading, questioning, probing. The result, I believe, has more than justified the effort.

Great outdoor literature endures for the same reason that any great art endures—it speaks to the timeless, to those aspects of human experience that transcend the trivial restrictions of time and place. Outdoor art has endured the longest through human history because it was first. Cave paintings depicting the hunt, hieroglyphs of the sun and the earth, crudely but lovingly drawn pictures of animals and birds—all signs of man's wonder at the mystery of his place in the world that is his home.

It was his first enemy and his first friend. He fought against nature for his very survival and then, in turn, worshiped its spirit, a spirit which man perceived as not unlike his own. And we've never lost that ancient paradox. We no longer hunt out of desperate necessity, yet we hunt nonetheless; we no longer develop religious dogma out of natural phenomena, yet we still can find in nature the surest window on ourselves.

This, of course, is the great theme of outdoor literature, the one that generations of writers have celebrated. Many in our century have failed and left behind little more than the endless tedium of how-to-do-it writing that is so easily and mercifully forgotten. But a few have caught that magic circle of man and the earth. Nash Buckingham, Corey Ford, Howard Walden, Burton Spiller, William Harnden Foster, Aldo Leopold—these men stand among the giants of outdoor literature and they stand so because they, best among their peers, have told us not only how we may be better outdoorsmen but in a far greater sense how we might be better men.

Now, the insights of our writers are more valuable than ever. And their task is different, because we face a prospect that no generation ever faced before. Human history is a chronicle of man's alteration of the earth, not always wisely nor always permanently, but with a grim determination that is irresistible. Now, for the first time, we can see the end of the wild, free earth. The end of home.

And not just wilderness. Home is simpler than that. Those who never have—and never will—set foot in real wilderness still cherish a fragment of home, whether it's a November cornfield in Iowa, a limestone stream in Pennsylvania, or a nameless slope a hundred miles out of Denver. It's the Ouachitas, the Smokies, a wild Minnesota lake, and the tamest bluegill pond in farmdom. It's where we feel free and at peace, where all the nicks and scratches on our busy minds and fretful hearts can heal.

A small corner of home disappears with every paved-over meadow, every bulldozed weedpatch, every dammed and strangled river. For our children and theirs, what we save may well be the measure of what we were.

But these, as John would say, are gray December thoughts. If home needs to be ministered, it also needs to be lived in, and this is more than anything else a book about living.

In choosing and assembling the chapters, I've kept sight of two of my fondest convictions. One is that no one stands closer to the heart and the spirit of the outdoors than the hunter. The other is that there is no voice that tells the hunter's story quite so well as John Madson's. This is a book about the hunter and the land and the creatures, told with the Madson magic: the tough, unsentimental love of the outdoors crafted into prose as straightforward as a spring-fed stream. He tells the old stories and makes them new again, the ageless stories of what is funny, sad, and wonderful in the fine and rugged landscape of home.

It's customary at this point to string out a list of people to whom thanks are due. For me, the list is brief but the feeling no less genuine. I owe the deepest gratitude to my friend John Madson, without whom this book would literally be at a loss for words; to Joel Vance for his unstinting help and encouragement and for being as fine a friend as anyone ever rode the river with; and to my wife Dana, to whose patience and affection I owe so much.

Michael McIntosh
Savannah, Missouri

Part I

OUT HOME

In touching every tree upon the hill,
The breath falls out of my voice,
And yet the singing keeps on.

James Dickey

Going Out More

OUR STATE CONSERVATION DEPARTMENT once made a special survey of hunters and what made them tick. About the only thing I can remember about it is how it related men's ages to their hunting efforts.

The average young hunter started out in his mid-teens, gunning up a storm. His hunting effort rose until he was in his early 20's, and then fell off. Of course it fell off. Chasing girls is a full-time project if it's done right.

Then, when he was in his late 20's, his hunting effort began to pick up again. Cabin fever, if we read the sign right. Our young hunter had married and settled down, the honeymoon was over, and Sugar Pie was on the nest and beginning to talk about painting the house. Time to dust off the old smokepole and head for the boondocks. From then on, hunting effort continued to climb through the hunter's 30's, leveling off in his 40's and declining slowly from then on as the old boy grew thick of girth and heavy of foot.

That's about how it's been with me. Today, at the half-century mark, I'm shocked to see how little hunting I am doing each fall and winter. I've been going out less, and I don't like it.

I'm still sound of wind and limb and can hoof it all day through grouse coverts and along the chukar slopes above the Snake. My shooting may even be better; what I've lost in reflexes and vision has been made up for in judgment and repression of buck fever. I'm now as cool on a covey rise as I may ever be.

But in the past few years much of my game hunting has been replaced with other types of hunting. The family has needed more money for college and that second car; there has been a growing responsibility at work. In a dozen ways, my hunting time and energy have been diverted into other channels — and none are as much fun as the old ones. So last fall marked the beginning of a personal revolt. There'll be some changes made. I'll be going out more.

My old highs will never be reached again, I know. I'll never have another 80-mallard season, or a 50-bird pheasant year. But I'm dam' well gonna do better than I have been!

Going out less has been due to a decline in my free time, not a decline in my free spirit. Under the grizzled wool of my bosom thumps the heart of a stripling nimrod. Last fall, before my first squirrel hunt of the season, I slept fitfully. And that was only a squirrel hunt, mind you! Before a deer hunt or grouse hunt—especially the ones I've traveled for—I hardly sleep at all. No, the old fever is still there. Give me a whiff of Hoppe's No. 9 and I'm hot to trot. It's the old freedom that's almost gone. I'm not really sure why. But I am sure that I haven't changed my mind about hunting itself.

I've been a hunter too long, both amateur and professional, to be driven from the field by slob hunters, intensified land use, antihunting sentiment or any decline of "free" hunting. Such things have existed ever since I can remember, and in my files are prophecies of doom from hunting magazines forty years old. When it comes to hunting, I'm a realist. I'm no Pollyanna, smiling through tears and offering the world my cookie. But I'm no Chicken Little, either, running about and crying that the sky is falling. Hunting has been around for a long time. It will be around for a long time to come, and will continue to offer the hunter as much as he's willing to search and work for.

The rising number of slob hunters may cramp my style, but they won't keep me at home. I've learned that the best way to avoid them is to simply avoid opening day, highly touted game areas, and the easy going. I hunt later on now, and more on the rough edges of the main action. This doesn't mean that my chances of finding game are greatly diminished; they may even be enhanced. I hunt better when I'm not crowded; being less hurried and not angry, I'm more inclined to hunt well. There are still special places I can find that will be mine—personal little corners of prime country that I've bought and paid for. Not with money, but by investing things that the slob hunter is rarely willing to spend. I learned long ago that good hunting is never free. It must always be paid for in some currency—maybe time, or effort, or even money. Maybe all three. And if there's one guy who really gravels me, it's the free-loader who demands prime hunting at no cost of any kind. Come to think of it, that's a good definition of the slob hunter.

I don't stay home because game habitat is shrinking, or because more hunters are gunning less land. There's still plenty of hunting to be had. On one weekend of Iowa pheasant hunting last fall, we asked eight farmers for hunting privileges. We were turned down only once—and on four of the other farms we were the only hunters who had been there! A couple of years ago we spent three days hunting ruffed grouse and never saw another hunter. Within twenty miles of my home I have hunting privileges on at least four farms, and in the past two years I haven't seen any other hunters on those places after quail, squirrels, rabbits, or deer.

Nor does any of the current antihunting fervor bother me. I understand my motives for hunting far better than my critics understand theirs—and I hold that my motives are more valid. Criticism of my sport might deter me if I had any real respect for antihunters. But as a professional wildlifer with nearly 40 years of hunting mileage, I just can't generate any real respect for my critics. The militant antihunters whom I have met lack real credentials, not just as hunters but as outdoorsmen. I'll listen to any antihunter who wears out a pair of field boots in two years' time—but I know none who do. The antihunters I've known are dabblers, and fair-weather outdoorsmen at best. Holding no respect for them, I am unmoved by their lack of respect for me. Having my life-style impugned by Alice Herrington or Cleveland Amory is like being run over by a baby buggy.

If I am hunting less, it isn't because I feel that the act of hunting degrades me or the creatures that are hunted. For me, the first measure of hunting isn't whether it is civilized, or conforms to suburban morality, but whether or not it jeopardizes the things that we hunt. If we hunt well, no game species is jeopardized. If we hunt badly, which is to say unethically or in ignorance, the species can be jeopardized and that is unforgivable. We must hunt so as to jeopardize no living species and in ways that shame neither hunter nor hunted.

I've known men who have hung up their guns, feeling that wildlife has enough problems without being hunted in the bargain. However, I feel a different sympathy for the animals—a sort of kinship that comes from sharing the same problems. As an elk or a bobwhite is endangered by habitat deterioration, so am I. But I know myself and the animals well enough to understand that my act of hunting makes little real difference. As those creatures are besieged by a pitiless technology, I know that they need me—the hunter. About all we have is each other. I wouldn't care to live in a world with no wild creatures or wild places left—and I suspect that the hunted animals may not be able to live without me, either. If my interest in hunting wanes and I hang up my gun, who will succor the wild creatures in the only ways that they really feel—by defending the little scraps of life range still left to them? As a hunter, I may be the only one that the wild creatures really have; and those wild creatures—biological indicators of the sort of quality environment that makes my life worth living—are all that I really have.

So my diminished hunting activity is not a sign of sentimental concern for wildlife. If I hunt less, it's not out of sympathy for the hunted; nor is it because I feel that I'm taking undue advantage of noble animals. If I'm sure of anything, it's this: That the act of ethical hunting is not an act of disrespect for the animal. Rather, it is a testimonial to that animal and what it stands for. It is a most genuine declaration of value. I do not hunt for the joy of killing but for the joy of living, and for the inexpressible pleasure of mingling my life, however briefly, with that of a wild creature that I respect, admire, and value. Then, too, I have a hunch that my act of hunting pays infinitely more respect to a game animal than if I stayed home and watched that animal perform on a television special.

Long ago I learned that my hunting is not just for meat, or horns, or recognition. It is a search for what hunting can give me, an effort to win once again that flash of insight that I have had a few times: That swift, sure intuition of how ancient hunters felt and what real hunting—honest-to-God *real* hunting—is all about. It is a timeless effort to close that magic circle of man, wildness and animal. Maybe, someday, I'll no longer have to go hunting to close that magic circle—but the day has not yet come.

What this adds up to, and what I'm missing most, is the freedom in hunting. Hunting is one of the last genuine, personal adventures of modern man. Just as game animals are the truest indicators of quality natural environment, so hunting is the truest indicator of quality natural freedom.

I once read of a noted physician who visited a northern deer camp for the first time. He wasn't a hunter, and it was all new to him. He stood by the cabin door one evening, watching some hunters dress deer while their buddies offered the ribald advice that you'll hear in a happy deer camp when the meat pole is heavy. Standing there, listening to the good laughter and the easy talk, the doctor turned to his host with a look of sudden understanding and said: "Why, these men are *free!*"

That's it. The real hunter is probably as free as it's possible for modern man to be in this teeming technocracy of ours. Not because he sheds civilized codes and restraints when he goes into the woods, becoming an animal, but because he can project himself out of and beyond himself and be wholly absorbed in a quieter, deeper and older world.

Another question I've asked myself: If I'm hunting less than I did, is it because I've found better outdoor things to do?

I try to savor every quality outdoor experience that I can. I canoe wild rivers, camp on desert islands in the southern sea, pack deep into remote wilderness by horse and foot, and these are all splendid things to do. My travels take me to some far, fair places. Come fall, however, and time for squirrels and .22s, I feel the old itch again. The feeling doesn't fade with the years; it deepens. And no amount of canoeing, hiking, exploring or fishing can really substitute for hunting.

It has occurred to me, of course, that I'd be better off not hunting. There's something to be said for staying at home in the fall. The nonhunter isn't likely to suffer charleyhorses, weariness, pain, hunger, cold, frustration, sleeplessness, and weekends away from home. His autumns are bland and peaceful. He doesn't neglect his family or drive his body beyond sensible limits, or invest money and time in equipment and travel that he can't afford. He takes autumn as it comes—a rich, mellow season highlighted by weekend football. By comparison, the genuine hunter is a flaky intransigent who starts coming unglued at the first turning leaf. To him, autumn isn't just another time of year—it's the reason why the rest of the year exists.

Awhile back, I asked an old friend in Arkansas' Boston Mountains if he planned any fall smallmouth fishing up on the Big Piney.

Pat considered this, and said:

"Aw, I reckon not. Come October, I start waitin' on birds."

"Pat, you know October is the best time to fish for smallmouths," I said.

"Sure it is," he replied, "and you know how I like to ketch them brown bass. But come fall, I'm obliged to wait on birds."

"But your quail season doesn't come in until early December."

"Which ain't my fault," Pat said thoughtfully. "Neither is bein' what I am. You know, I wouldn't go to hell to shoot a quail, but I'd mess around the edge until I fell in."

For men like that, the long wait until hunting season is like the long night before opening day. They are restless, tossing and turning and waiting for first light—or autumn. Their lives would be more placid and serene without hunting. But then, the churchyards are filled with serene, placid men who do not hunt.

It all adds up to this, an ancient Roman inscription in a ruined forum near Timgad, Algeria: "To bathe, to talk, to laugh, to hunt—this is to live."

Bathing I've been getting a lot of. But with no more hunting than I've had lately, I don't have much to talk or laugh about. That's done with. Next season I'll be going out more, going out home again.

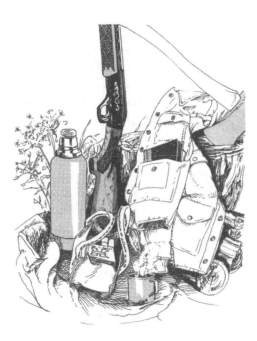

An Outdoor Ledger

THE YEARS AFIELD HAVE LED ME TO DISCARD many of the things that I've been told about the outdoors in general and hunting in particular, and it sometimes seems that I'm almost back where I started.

But if I don't know as much as I should at this late date, what I do know is pretty much for *sure*.

My meager store of hunting wisdom, for example, gathered over decades of boondocking and chore-dodging, falls into four general categories:

People
1. A hunting partner usually oversleeps.
2. A wife sleeps deepest when her duckhunter wants his breakfast.
3. The guys in the next duck blind are no good.
4. Beware the quick shooter, for thou shalt inherit his quickly shot birds.
5. Blessed be the camp cook, the wife who cleans game, and the partner with two candy bars.

Equipment
1. A knife can't be too sharp.
2. Hip boots leak only in cold water.
3. When matches are fewest, firewood is wettest.
4. For a drippy nose, a wool mitten beats any bandana.
5. Never be the only man in the party with a game pocket in his hunting coat.

Critters
1. Foxes are not fit to eat.
2. As long as a duck is still coming toward you, shut up and don't call.
3. Squirrels can't lie still for over 20 minutes.
4. I can't sit still for over 19 minutes.
5. Geese are not smart. They are just smarter than most hunters.

Other Things
1. Fences are always two inches higher than my legs.
2. Your shot was lucky; mine was skillful.
3. Only the men who build farm gates can really understand them.
4. Bird dogs are optimists; pheasants are pessimists.
5. There is no greater nor more touching faith than a small boy's defense of his birdless dad.
6. The last hills are the highest.

These are the only hunting facts that I'm dead sure of, for I've never seen exceptions to any of them. There's lots of stuff that I'm half-sure of. It's fairly certain that wives save up the year's odd jobs for October, and that small boys like to carry rabbits or empty shotshells just as much as they ever did.

I'm also pretty sure that although the outdoor life is milestoned with 12-point bucks and other spectaculars, it is essentially a sum of the small things—the swarm of trivia that provides the most durable delights and exasperations.

Among the latter, top billing might go to stinging nettle, deerflies lighting in your hair, chocolate bars that melt in the pocket, bulls along favorite streams, sentinel crows, rainy Saturdays, clay mud, wormy walnuts, algae on fishing ponds, hot opening days, cold opening days, broken glass on sandbars, the setter-cockleburr combination, seed ticks in bellybuttons, dead fishworms, catfish spines, and cross farm dogs.

Just about as bad are game hogs, moonshooters, bellyachers, poor camp cooks, barbershop biologists, phony outdoorsmen in television commercials, and kids that throw rocks where you're fishing.

The least inspiring outdoor activities are digging goose pits in bottomland gumbo, washing frypans in April trout streams, breaking camp, getting up before dawn in the rain, stepping on snakes, and sleeping cold.

On the other side of the ledger are the good things: cedar waxwings and cedar sawdust and cedar turkey calls and canoes, wild strawberries, morel mushrooms, dragonflies on fishing lines, flat stones for skipping on water, old light bulbs around dumps when you're plinking, campfires that last all night and mosquitos that don't, clearing skies, and fish that strike on the first cast of the day.

People I'd like to see more of are low pressure sporting goods salesmen, game wardens, friendly farmers, fishing partners who know Robert Service's poems by heart, wives who can clean fish, and women who don't cringe from snakes. The best smells are onion soup in an icefishing shanty, woodsmoke in town, balsam air, morning coffee, and snow wind blowing down from glaciers across fields of alpine flowers.

Some of the most congenial outdoor labors are nightcrawler hunting, finding arrowheads, walking barefoot on wet sand, putting on dry socks, chewing watercress, building a fire in the rain with only one match, and spitting off high bridges into water.

There are two times that are best.

One is when you're thirteen years old, walking home with your .22 and three rabbits and meeting the prettiest girl in the seventh grade.

The other is the cruel winter evening when you're about done in and you see the kitchen window of home glowing across crusted snow, and you walk down a path of lamplight to where mother is waiting supper.

Partner, that'll get it when it's almost gone!

Dallas Morgan
and the Lion

WE WERE IN ELK CAMP WITH NIGHT COMING ON and the young bull of
the afternoon was quartered and hung in the quakers behind the
tent. Supper was over and we were taking our ease by the fire,
full of Joe's biscuits and fresh elk liver and gravy.

Off yonder, Solomon Creek was brawling through its deep
canyon under the Wyoming line. The temperature was falling
again and there was the smell of more snow in the air, but it was
a snug enough camp with plenty of straw under the tent and
firewood put by.

There was the sound of a pickup on the road, laboring along
in all-wheel drive. It stopped, a door closed quietly, and a
Colorado conservation officer stepped into the firelight. Our old
friend Dallas Morgan looked real spiffy in his Class A uniform.
The glass of fashion and the mold of form, as they say. We told
him so, apologizing for our whiskers and dirty pants. Dallas
cussed mildly at that and helped himself to the coffee and
biscuits.

He squatted Indian-fashion beside the fire, a compact man in his early sixties and nearing retirement from the Department. Unlike many old riders he was not saddle-bowed nor stiffened by old hurts, and moved easily and lightly. His face was deeply lined and cured by a lifetime of sun and wind, but it was the eyes that caught and held attention—flat, hard eyes that always seemed to see beyond what they were looking at.

We sat there in the circle of light—the night trying to get in but held at bay by the fire—and the talk turned, as it always does, to other times and other hunts. Someone asked Dallas how many elk he had killed.

"Not many. Some. Most of my real huntin', the trail huntin', has been for lions."

"How many lions, then?"

"Seventy-six. I kept track because most of them were taken in control work, mostly in the old days."

"That's a bunch of mountain lions," someone said. "Kill all of 'em in the chickenhouse?"

"There, and down in the catnip patch," Dallas grinned. "All except one, mebbee."

We waited. Dallas paused, looking into the fire and remembering, and then told about it.

You know that I come up from west Texas in '27, and that fall my brother Frank and I went fur-trapping over by Gunnison. Camped out all that winter and made us $4,400, and in those days that would buy a mess of groceries. Well, that got me started, and a few years later I went to work for the old Bureau of Biological Survey as a government hunter.

I worked for the government off and on for about fifteen years, mostly trapping bears and coyotes when I started out. But even then I was hunting some lions on my own, and usually had a good dog or two.

Along in the middle 1930s reports started comin' in to my boss in Grand Junction about a big old tom lion that was giving stockmen some trouble. This lion would leave the Utah border country every spring and head up east to the Grand Mesa. He'd follow the deer herd up out of winter range right back to the top of the mesa and stay there until the blizzards run the deer back down again and he'd go with them. Coming or going, the old devil would usually pick off a colt or two on the way. Mountain lions love horseflesh, and this old boy had a taste for thorough-bred stock.

For five-six years the boss had put hunters on that cat, but none of 'em had done any good. Something always went wrong; the lion would get to where men and dogs couldn't follow, or the weather went bad, or something. I kept after the boss, saying: "Why don't you send me after that cat? I'll get him for you!" And he'd say: "Morgan, what makes you think you got something them other hunters ain't got?" And I'd tell him: "Well, I got a dog that they ain't got, and I got guts enough to foller him to the end of the trail and come back with his head and hide, *that's* what I got!"

It was along in late March, 1941, that he called me on the telephone and said: "Well, you been braggin' for three or four years about what a hell of a lion hunter you are, so jest throw your grub box and a bedroll in your truck and come down to Grand Junction and I'll draw you a map and tell you where to pick up that lion's trail."

I took off like a rabbit. But when I got back home fourteen days later, I wasn't running like a rabbit, let me tell you.

My lead dog was an old black-and-tan hound named Tige. His mother hadn't been much, but I'd bred her to a real good trail dog that I had—and then danged if I didn't lose her up in the mountains one time. She showed up later at a road camp down in the Dry Creek Basin, and whelped just one pup. That was Tige. The road boss knew I'd lost her and he called me, and I went down and brought home the pup. Left the bitch with the road boss—he wanted her because she was pretty good at trail-ing wild horses. Well, that Tige was about five months old when I got him, and many years old when he went under. He was a fine dog, a great dog. I never hope to have a better one. The two pups, Singer and Brownie, were also black-and-tans but only a couple of years old. They were coming along pretty well, though.

I wasn't taking a horse. Oh, I've used horses on lion hunts but I don't like it much. They'll save you a lot of yardage once in a while, but a man and dogs can go places where no horse can go and if you have to picket a horse and leave him back in that rough country, there's no telling when you'll get back to him. So this hunt was gonna be on foot, slow-trailin', just me and those three hounds.

A man named Tom Kelley was ranching up north of Mack, and he'd called my boss to tell him that his Spanish sheepherder had seen the lion going through their place four or five days previous. After getting my bearings at Grand Junction, I headed up to the Kelley spread at the mouth of Achee Canyon.

I got there on the first of April. I'd planned on driving up into the canyon and fooling round until dark trying to cut some sign, and then coming back to the ranch to talk to the herder. But when I got there I found that a landslide had closed the dirt road, so I left the truck, grabbed the dogs, and headed up in there on foot. Never did cut that lion's trail, though, and ended up in a little line shack under the rim, sleeping on some bare bedsprings, which is an awful poor way to sleep. Got back down to Kelley's ranch the next afternoon.

The Mex herder told me that I hadn't gone far enough up-country, and pointed out the place where the lion had crossed the canyon five nights before. He'd heard the cat scream and figured he was probably up behind a high point we were look-ing at, and headed east. The old man warned me about a certain place up there, and told me to hold in the dogs when I got to it. Said a hog had died up there, and he filled the pig full of strychnine and buried it in loose sand under a rimrock that the lion always went under when he crossed that country.

I left the truck down there at the end of the road and stuck a piece of paper under the windshield wiper, saying: "Dallas Morgan went that way on April 2," with an arrow pointing east.

Well, I found the place where the hog had been buried, and danged if the lion hadn't gone in under the rimrock and dragged it out, but it was already bloated and stinkin' and the lion wouldn't eat it. That's right where I picked up his tracks, and he had a long start on me. Away we went.

It was pretty rough country right in there, and it got a whole lot worse. Great, high rimrock, and cedar and piñon mountainsides and long, high hogbacks. With that one big main rim that runs all through that country, that you can see all the way from Grand Junction. There were lots of shale cliffs, and sometimes I'd cross long stretches of open rock, and other times I'd be high up, in stands of pines and quakers. It was country where long hogbacks ran down from the main rim, and this cat was traveling dead east, up and down across those hogbacks. And here and there the country would just stand up on its hind legs, with red-and-yellow sandstone walls hundreds of feet high, capped with cedar and piñon. No sign of people at all, and the farther we went into that country the rougher it got.

I've never seen country any wilder. I was some hoss back in those days, but even so I got a little edgy. I don't care what anybody says, a man's a fool to go into places like that alone— time and again I was where a slip would have put me through three hundred feet of thin air, along narrow ledges, up and over rotten shale cliffs—all sorts of places where a man could get killed. Or bust a leg, which comes to the same thing.

About every day I'd find a big old cedar snag, an old dead tree away from the rest of the timber, and I'd set that old tree afire. In this day and age they'd have me in jail, leaving an unattended fire, but I'm in the roughest country that I'd ever laid eyes on and I wanted to leave sign so somebody could trail me and at least find my bones in case something happened. So most every day I'd set an old tree afire, and when I'd hit some high ground I would look back and see those spirals of smoke, away off to the west behind me.

I was traveling mighty light. No choice. Had a little old Monkey Ward packsack and a single wool blanket that I'd bought on credit at a Spiegel store. For grub I had plenty of oatmeal and a little sugar and coffee, some dried chipped beef and Zweiback toast, with a frypan and coffee pot and a little lard. I sure ate lots of oatmeal; it doesn't weigh much, you know. Even so, I ended up losing eleven pounds on that trip—and it was weight that I didn't have to spare.

Late each day, when I'd see that there was no chance of

jumpin' that cat and turnin' the dogs loose on him, I'd quit ahead of sundown—and by that time, my hind parts wouldn't be six inches off the ground, anyway. I'd hunt up a place under a ledge where I could get some shelter, and drag wood up there and build a big fire. I'd heat up some slabs of rock and then dig a hole in the sand and push the rocks into it and cover 'em up with sand again. That's where I'd sleep, and it stayed warm quite a while. It was below freezing every night and I'd get a little chilly before daylight, but I'd wake up and build up the fire again and go back to sleep. Trouble was, when the fire would heat the back wall of rock, all the bugs would start thinkin' it was summer and come out of the cracks.

One night, along in the wee hours, something bit me on the ham, *kerbang*! I rolled out of the blanket trying to jerk off those tight Levis, and shook 'em and out rolled a big old gray spider the size of a two-bit piece. Didn't know what else to do, so I chewed up a cigarette and made a mash of it and held it on that bite until the tobacco got dry. It was a hard place to get to and doctor myself, but you know, that bite never even itched afterward.

All night long I could feel those three dogs shivering up against me. Come morning they could hardly stand up, they were so stiff, and after five or six days the pads of their feet were wearing down to the quick, worn off on the rock we were traveling on. Old Tige would stand up and stretch and whine, and the two pups would generally just lay there and several mornings I had to cut a switch and make 'em get out of their beds and take the trail. The days were sunny and the snow was mostly gone by then, but down in the deep canyons and on some of the north slopes there were still old snowbanks.

I got to know that lion's track real well. We cut other lion trails from time to time, and once we saw sign of a peg-legged lion, but there was no mistaking the track of the old tom we were after. He had big pads, anyway five inches across, and they were scarred and creased and cracked like an old hound's.

Sometimes we would pick up his trail along dirt paths or in sandy washes, or in dust under big ledges. We would trail him pretty fast then, but we'd always hit high ledges or long stretches of bare rock. Most of my lion hunting has been on some snow, and going in there in early April was doing it the hard way. The lion knew where he was goin', and we didn't. He knew just where he was heading—and he knew where every break in those big walls was. He knew right where the deer fed and bedded down for the night; he had favorite places where he traveled on or under long ledges, sometimes for a long ways across bare rock. Many times he went into places where I couldn't follow. You know, a man can go where a dog can't, especially up. And I always had to think of my dogs—I couldn't go anyplace where they couldn't follow me. When that old lion would come to a long, narrow ledge up on a high wall, me and the dogs would have to try to dope out where he'd come down, and then take the long way around and cut sign on the other side someplace.

We'd lose his trail for hours at a time. Especially along that high rim and in those big walls, with just solid rock and a few scraggly trees growing there. I'd never turn the dogs loose, but always kept them with me. But when we came to places like that, I'd put Tige out ahead of me and like as not he'd hit a place where the lion had brushed against a tree limb, or against a rock, and Tige would smell it and throw back his head and give a bawl you could hear halfway to Grand Junction, and I knew we were still on the route.

It was worse when we were just starting out. In five days' time at that month of the year, on dry ground, a dog can't help you much except when a lion rubs against something. But between me spotting his padmarks on dirt and sand, and Tige getting a whiff of him now and then on rock ledges, we kept to his trail. And if Tige was up ahead a ways and got to working a little too fast, I'd speak to him and he'd stop where he was and wait until I passed him up, and he'd fall in behind me and we'd keep going ahead.

Now and then we'd cut other sign. Sometimes we'd find some of his scratch sign—lions are about like a wolf or coyote, and use the same latrines year after year. This lion was old and smart, traveling mostly up in the high rocks where he could look back down on the country he'd come through; he didn't spend much time down in the low washes except to cross them.

We were finding dead deer, too, killed along cedar benches or back in timbered pockets. They were fresh kills and getting fresher, most of them with just one good meal eaten out of them. In nine days' time we come across nine deer that the lion had killed. He might scratch a little dirt or some piñon needles over a deer, but he never really covered it up the way a lion will if he intends to come back. That old cat was just living off the land as he went, and he kept going pretty steady. All along his line of travel I found piles of old deer bones that I was pretty sure he had accounted for. I reckon it would be real surprising, if a man had a way of knowing just how many deer that old cat had sacked up in that country. I fed some of that deer meat to my dogs but didn't eat any myself. The deer were winter-poor and pretty stringy, but Tige and the pups didn't mind. They were eatin' better than I was, at that.

One of the things that helped out with the tracking was the fact that there wasn't much disturbance on any of that ground. No cattle at all, and mostly I was just seeing wild horse sign and deer tracks. Why, I put my feet into places where I know there'd never even been an Indian. I saw no human sign, new or old, of any kind. Except for one night toward the end, when we slept under a deep rim and there were four or five unbroken Indian pots lined up against the back wall.

We weren't going very fast, probably not making more than fifteen miles a day with all that slow-trailin'. Time and again, for hours on end, we'd lose the trail on long sheets of bare rock or up in those high sandstone walls, and we'd have to cut out ahead or off to the side to pick up the trail somewhere else. It was a long, slow job. A mountain lion is a terrible beast in rough country; he can climb better than any squirrel, and if he don't want you to follow him he can go into places that you bloody well can't git to. Still, I don't reckon the lion even knew we were on his trail that first week. He was killing his meat most every night, and laying up in the daytime, and we were gaining on him some. But he shore wasn't wanderin' much; he was just goin' where he'd gone many times before, and taking the most direct way to get there. He was taking us up to the Grand Mesa, up to his summer huntin' range, and we had our work cut out for us.

It must have been sundown on the sixth day, when I was making camp under a big old ledge and looked across the canyon and saw some deer on a cedar bench over there. They were flicking their tails and fooling around and acting pretty spooky, and I knew right then that there was a lion right close—and I had a hunch that we were gonna jump that big tom the next day.

Come morning, I found where the lion had been hunting those deer the night before. Plenty of sign, but he hadn't made his kill. We came up to a place where his tracks showed that he was running, and that was the first time on the hunt that I really turned Tige loose. Off he tore, hot on that trail, the pups right behind him.

The lion couldn't have been far ahead, and he gave the dogs a hard, fast run that took them along a big cedar bench, up into the breaks of the high walls and right up on top of the main rim. By the time I got up there with them, they were at the edge of the rim baying their heads off, and you could see that the lion had just gone right on over.

It was a big smooth face of rock that slanted and curved off down out of sight. I couldn't see much, but I knew that lion was down there someplace and I could see what mebbee looked like a ledge off below. Only one thing to do. I took off my boots (what was left of 'em) and that Monkey Ward packsack and sat down and slid off over that bulge of rock. I had no way of knowin' how much of a ledge was down there, but I had a lot of confidence in that old lion. He knew that country better than anything living, and if he testified that there was a place to stand on down there, why, I'd believe him!

I was just picking up speed, sliding, when I hit the ledge. It wasn't much—only about as wide as my foot is long, and I wear a number nine boot. From there on down, it was a smooth wall for at least a hundred feet to the rocks. Well, I edged along for

fifteen feet or so until I came to a sharp corner out of sight of the
dogs above. The ledge went around that corner at right angles,
and I reached out and grabbed the sharp edge of that rock corner
with my hand and stuck my head around. *Waugh*! There was the
lion, just around that corner a few feet away, and as soon as he
saw me he spat and jumped.

I almost went, too. I could feel my shoulders leave the rock
wall behind me, and the rifle almost overbalanced me. Oh,
Lordy, I *almost* went! It was an awful near thing, and for a second
there I was just teeterin' between this world and the next. But I
caught my balance, and plastered myself up against that wall
like a fly. The cat had jumped straight down about twenty feet
into the top of an enormous dead pine that was leaning up
against the canyon wall on his side, and I could hear the dead
limbs crashing and busting all the way down until he hit the
rock slide below. And when they heard that, and probably
smelled him, too, the dogs up above really went wild.

Well, I worked back the other way and finally found a place
that I could climb up into and get back on top and get my boots
and packsack. It took us an hour or more to find our way back
down below the rim, and when we finally got there we could see
that the cat had really taken off—he was makin' a lot of fast
tracks to the east. That had been the first time that he'd even
known I was in the same world with him, and he was shook up
some. So was I. Got a real close look at him up there and he was
one helluva tom lion, let me tell you.

No way we could catch up to him that day—not with the
flyin' head start that he had, and with dark comin' on. So, we
found us a place in the rimrock and built a fire and shut down
for the night.

Just before full dark when we'd quit the lion's trail, I saw a big
old hogback off to the east in the direction the cat was headin'.
There was a real low saddle in that hogback, and I went to sleep
figuring that it was a logical place for the lion to cut through.

Next morning I figured I'd just take a loop over there to see
what was what, and decided to leave the dogs tied up where we
had spent the night. The dogs were awful footsore, and their

nails were almost gone. So were my boots, as a matter of fact. That tough country was tearing the soles off. Anyway, I left the dogs behind and headed toward that hogback to see if I could cut the lion's trail and get things started again. I went on up the mountain for four or five miles, up into that saddle, and was partway through it when danged if I didn't jump that lion from under a ledge of rock!

He took out of there pretty fast, turning back and heading off west the way he'd come. And I figured: "Why, I'll just shoot that old boy!" So I took out after him, trailing until sundown. Took me quite a while to get up on that mountain with him, and his trail led to a place where there was a sort of island of big broken rocks, a devil of a tough place that covered three acres or so. His tracks went around this big old rockpile and I followed them and by the time I come back to where I'd started, I found fresh padmarks in my own footprints. He was stepping right in my tracks, following me around that big rockpile.

I know that mountain lions ain't supposed to attack men. Been hearing that all my life. But try to tell that to yourself when you're up there alone on a mountain that's 'way off to hell and gone, with the light going fast, and a big old scarred lion walking in your footprints—an old tom that knows you're hunt- in' him. A lone man hunting *him*, the king of the mesas, on his own ground! I didn't care for that a whole lot. So I didn't backtrack the way I'd come up because I didn't want to meet that big tom in the dark, but instead cut off to the south down- mountain for a quarter-mile or so and picked up the contour and headed back to the dogs. I built a mighty fast fire, I'll tell you.

Well, I was back up there with the dogs at first light, and saw where the lion had trailed me for a ways back down the moun- tainside the night before. He'd followed me just minutes after I'd left that pile of rock. I began to work his track then, and Tige was hitting fresh scent and knew it. My old lead dog could probably have taken the trail and run the lion right then if I'd let him, but I was afraid the dogs would get so far away that I couldn't hear them when the cat treed. So I made Tige and the pups keep in there behind me and I kept tracking the lion by sign. It was a day I'll never forget—the morning of the 13th day since I'd left home.

After he'd quit my track the night before, the lion had turned back to the right and gone to huntin' in those cedar benches and draws. The old dog began gettin' awful excited and wanted to get past me and get on that track himself, and about then we came up on a doe deer that the lion had killed the night before. He'd cut down behind her shoulder and eaten her lights, and it hadn't been too awful long before.

Past that dead deer there was solid rock for about a quarter-mile, so I had to put old Tige to work on that and it was a job keepin' that dog from goin' too fast. Well, it was gettin' pretty warm on that big south mountainside by the middle of April, and when we finally jumped the lion he had been layin' on his belly in a big old snowbank. We didn't see him go, but when we came up there I could see where he'd been and the way he'd unsheathed his claws to get a flyin' jump off that snowbank, and I knew that we were right behind him. That's when I turned the dogs loose, on a trail that was stinkin' hot. Clapped my hands and yelled: "*Go git that old sonofabitch!*"

Like that other time, the lion headed for the high ground up above the main rim. I wasn't far behind Tige when he got up there, but had no idea where the pups were. No sign of 'em. They were still down there someplace below, tryin' to git up.

When I got up to the top I could hear my old dog real plain. I'd come up into this big open park that was full of sagebrush and a few trees and I was watching it, thinking that the way Tige was comin' on, he'd cross that park just behind the lion.

Well, I didn't get there in time. The lion had already gone through. And there was one tree kind of settin' out there by itself and I could see something that was a different color than the pine needles and such, and I thought it was that big old yaller cat up there. But I saw my dog sailin' past that tree without slowin' down, so I cocked my eyes off to the right and there was one more tree a few hundred yards from the regular timbered country and about as far from the main rim. And in that tree there was just a fair picture of a lion settin'. I just knew it had to be that old tom.

Tige sailed in under that tree goin' about forty knots, went thirty or forty jumps past the tree and then just slid on his hind end and turned around and went in under the tree a second time. He ran up to the trunk of the tree and put his front feet up on it and gave that old treed bark that I knew meant: "Here he is, boss, come and git him!" By looking straight up through the limbs he couldn't see the lion, so he'd run back a ways and set down where he could see the cat, put his head up again, and go to bayin'.

Reckon I was about 300 yards away and it was mostly open country between me and that tree. I was afraid that if the lion saw me comin' he might bail out of there and get back over to that awful big cliff again that I didn't *ever* want him to git back to, so I tried to sneak—keepin' boulders in front of me, crawlin' and first one thing or two, until I finally run plumb out of cover. I'd judge I was about 75 yards from the tree then, and figured: "Boy, if you can't hit him from here with that rifle, you might as well git a handful of rocks."

So I got a good solid rest and let fly, and knew the second I'd touched it off that I'd scored a lick. The lion didn't fall, but he swung around and began grabbin'. I took another quick shot and down through the limbs he come. As soon as Tige saw him fallin', he went for the trunk of that tree and the lion lit right by him and got up on his feet and ran, swingin' one shoulder, and Tige reached up and grabbed him by the ham and that's the last thing I saw—that lion draggin' Tige over the top of the steep hillside toward that big rim.

When I got over there I could hear Tige bawling somewhere downslope. There was this steep hillside running back from the main rim, and a big old pine had uprooted itself from the hill and fallen down and was hanging out over the cliff. There was the lion out on that log. He'd turned himself around and kind of wedged that broken shoulder in the fork of a limb and had the other foot drawed back. Tige had followed him out there and was laying on his belly on the log about three feet from the lion's face, the slobber just a-flyin', and when old Tige would stick out his neck and beller and boom, that lion would take a swipe at him. I thought: "Lord, if he ever hooks my dog in the jaw with that big foot it'll be the end of Tige!" And just about that time I heard the two pups comin' into the far end of the meadow up above. They'd made their turn and hit Tige's and the lion's tracks and here they come, screamin' their fool heads off.

Now, this was a north slope and there was still ice under the pine needles on that steep hillside. And I knew that at the speed they were comin', those pups would run right off the cliff. They'd hit that icy slope with those pine needles dusted over it, and could never stop.

But in the meantime there was Tige out there on that dam' log fixin' to git himself killed by that old tom lion. So I got down there on the log and eased up behind my dog and got him by the tail, stuck that .250 Savage just over the top of Tige's head, and shot the lion. He turned loose all holds and fell. I cocked my ear to hear him hit, and it seemed like a full minute before I heard the crash 'way down below. That big sandstone wall was three hundred feet high if it was an inch. And here come the pups!

I backed off the log, pullin' Tige by the tail, and had just got on solid ground and was wavin' my arms when the pups came over the top of the hill. The front dog went tearing past me and saw what he was about to do, and stuck all four feet in the ground and started slidin', tryin' to turn, and his hindparts swing off the cliff. There he hung, his worn-down front claws in that icy dirt tryin' to get hold, and his hind legs clawing at that sandstone wall. No way that I could help him, or I'd have gone over too. He'd finally hook a claw in the sandstone and push himself up and the foot would give way and he'd jest *nearly* slide off. Boys—I reckon that was the most exciting five minutes of my whole life, right there.

When that part of it was over and I got my wind back, I crawled back out on that log and went to lookin' for the lion. Night was comin' on and it was hard to see down there, but I finally spotted him layin' down there on his back in a little dry wash and he didn't look any bigger than a coyote.

It took about an hour and a half to get down there to where he was; I was quite a ways from where I'd come up and that rim got

some tougher, climbing back down in the dark. I had to build a
big bonfire for light to skin that lion by. That was back in the
days with us workin' for the government when we had to bring
in the head and hide of every lion to prove up. I skinned him
out, cut off the head, and rolled head and pelt into a load and
got out of there. I'd had my fill of rimrockin' for a spell, and
made up my mind that I was gonna sleep in a bed someplace if I
had to walk all night.

It was the biggest lion that I ever took, and I reckon he was
the biggest I've ever seen.

One time I weighed another lion that was a little over nine
feet long in the carcass and scaled at 198 pounds. And that's a
whole bunch of cat to be wrapped up in one hide, I'll tell you.
Well, this one was at least as long and heavy as that other. A
record? I don't know; we never measured the skull. No reason
for us to. But he was nine feet, three inches long. His ears were
split and chewed on, and there were old scars all over his face.
He'd been in a lot of fights tryin' to stay boss of the woods, and
I reckon that he'd been boss until the end.

My brother Frank, who knew that country fairly well, figured
out that I'd hunted just about seventy miles from where I first
parked my truck at the mouth of Achee Canyon. Don't know
what it would have been if it was ironed out flat. But that's far
enough for any lion, even one that big.

I've taken a lot of lions since then, and followed some hard
trails, but that was the main one, I reckon. Always will be, for
me. And I done it in a way that I like to remember, by trailin' on
foot, with no poison. That's how a cat like that should be taken,
with a man and a good dog against him in his home range, up
there in the rims with man and dog and lion all doin' their best,
and nothin' to be ashamed of no matter how it comes out.

Times have changed. The old days of tryin' to wipe out every
lion in the country are over, and it's just as well. They're game
animals now in most places and that's the way it should be, for
they're as game as any animal ever was. There'll always be a few
lions that get to takin' livestock and I reckon they've got to be
stopped, but that's no reason to make war on the whole tribe.

Almost gone? Not by a jugful! There are still plenty of lions back in those old rims. Hope there always will be, with plenty of deer for 'em to hunt. They're all part of the same thing, part of the mountains and the way things were. And if tomorrow's gonna be worth a dam', they'll be part of that, too.

Palace
in the Popple

It's a smoky, raunchy boars' nest
  With an unswept, drafty floor
And pillowticking curtains
  And knife scars on the door.
The smell of a pine-knot fire
  From a stovepipe that's come loose
Mingles sweetly with the bootgrease
  And the Copenhagen snoose.

There are work-worn .30-30s
  With battered, steel-shod stocks
And drying lines of longjohns
  And of steaming, pungent socks.
There's a table for the Bloody Four
  And their game of two-card draw,
And there's deep and dreamless sleeping
  On bunk ticks stuffed with straw.

Jerry and Jake stand by the stove,
   Their gun-talk loud and hot,
And Bogie has drawn a pair of kings
   And is raking in the pot.
Frank's been drafted again as cook
   And is peeling some spuds for stew
While Bruce wanders by in baggy drawers
   Reciting "Dan McGrew."

No where on earth is fire so warm
   Nor coffee so infernal
Nor whiskers so stiff, jokes so rich,
   Nor hope blooming so eternal.
A man can live for a solid week
   In the same old underbritches
And walk like a man and spit where he wants
   And scratch himself where he itches.

I tell you, boys, there's no place else
   Where I'd rather be, come fall,
Where I eat like a bear and sing like a wolf
   And feel like I'm bull-pine tall.
In that raunchy cabin out in the bush
   In the land of the raven and loon,
With a tracking snow lying new to the ground
   At the end of the rutting moon.

The Secret Life
of the Cottontail Deer

IF THERE'S ANYTHING DULL ABOUT A WHITETAIL DEER, I don't know it. I like everything about him. His biology is fascinating. So is his management, his history, and the old legends and grandpa yarns. I like to talk about whitetails with hunters, and with such seasoned deer men as Jack Calhoun of Illinois and Bill Severinghaus of New York. I admire a deer rifle that shoots true and handles easy. I've got a hunch that good tracking snow and prime roast venison may just help a man live forever. And as the years go by, I become more and more absorbed with the essence of the whitetail—the cunning thing inside that makes him what he is.

The whitetail is the only big-game animal that has succeeded in our woodlots and field edges, and he's made it because he's sharp. His senses of smell and hearing are acute beyond belief, and his vision is probably as keen as ours even though it's in black and white.

His success, however, doesn't just depend on the sensory information that he soaks up but on the ways that he plugs it in. Those keen senses detect the slightest changes in the deer's

home range. And how he knows that home range! He knows
every little break in terrain, the open ground and its edges, each
windfall, thicket, rootwad, spring seep, berry tangle, cutbank,
and mire. No human hunter can possibly know the deer range as
well.

Knowing that range, and sensing an alien presence there, the
whitetail reacts in many ways. He may lie doggo, watchful and
waiting, or sneak catlike around an intruder. He may explode
into action, white banner astern, making spectacular leaps over
obstacles and racing headlong through heavy timber—only to
stop somewhere just beyond and fade into a thicket off to one
side to resume lurking and spying. He has a particular genius for
melting into cover that couldn't possibly conceal a deer.

A few years back, my old friend Keith Kirkpatrick was on a
whitetail hunt with several friends. They were driving some
farm timber known to have deer, but they hadn't seen any. One
of the group, a young man who had never hunted deer, asked
the farmer where the deer were. The farmer didn't know, but he
figured that somebody ought to hunt a brushy draw that ran
from the timber out into the fields.

The hunter worked through this cover, coming out into an
open field where there was a little pond. It didn't look like
much. But as he stood there wondering what to do, he heard
quail chirping in the fringe of foxtail and sloughgrass. He
shucked the deer slugs from his shotgun, slipped in some bird
loads, and stepped into the grass. The covey roared up. And at
the same instant a big buck broke cover a few yards away. He
tore across the fields and vanished, leaving our hero with a gun
full of bird loads and egg on his face.

It was a standard whitetail trick. We should be used to it by
now, especially out in the Midwest where good deer populations
thrive in woodlots, thin fringes of creek brush, and all manner of
little cover scraps. Still, it's always a surprise to find deer there.
Even more surprising are the people who share their land with
these superb animals and never know it.

There was a certain place in central Iowa where I usually
could count on a pheasant or two late in the season—a little
dimple in the rolling farmland that couldn't be seen by road

hunters. It was in the exact center of the mile-square land
section, half a mile from any road, the remnant of an old farm
dump that was set about with sumac and undergrown with giant
foxtail.

I hunted up to it one day in late December, working into the
wind on an inch of snow. By the time I was within gun range of
the little covert I could sense that empty, birdless quality that a
long-time pheasant hunter learns. But I played out the hand
anyway. I stood in the fence corner for a couple of minutes,
looking things over, knowing that this might do as much to
flush a hiding rooster as any cover-kicking. Nothing. I jacked
open the Model 12 and swung up on the fence.

He came to his feet in one fluid, powerful movement and was
instantly on his way with that buoyant grace that even very
large whitetails have. He had been lying beside a roll of rusty
fencewire, his antlers melting into the sumac around him. He
couldn't have been 50 feet from me. If he'd been a pheasant's
head I might have seen him. I was hunting pheasants. I hadn't
expected anything like him.

I knew him for what he was. I was a professional wildlifer by
that time. In fact, I had just finished working at the Lansing
check station for five days, and we had weighed and aged many
deer, including a dozen bucks that would take any hunter's
breath away. But nothing like this one.

His broad back looked as if it might hold water in a heavy
rain, the gray neck seeming as thick as a Holstein bull's. He wore
a typical rack, though I haven't the slightest idea of how many
points there were. It was the sheer weight of antler that stays in
my mind. Between burr and brow tine each main beam was as
thick as my wrist, arching out and forward in great curves, with
broad webbing where the tines arose. Ten days before we had
weighed a buck that would have gone 250 pounds, and this one
was bigger.

He rose weightless out of his bed and ran off down the fence
line, making no sound that I can remember. It was easily the
largest whitetail I had ever seen. He left me there on the fence,
heart pounding, breath coming short, and legs trembling.

I casually asked two farmers living on that square mile if

they'd seen any deer around, especially anything big. Yeah, they'd seen a few deer earlier but the hunters must have killed them all. I told the local game warden, a good friend. He was keenly interested, but hadn't seen such a buck nor heard of anyone who had. Same with several good local hunters.

That deer was probably never taken by a hunter. There'd have been no keeping it out of the record books. Nor was he killed on a road during the antlerless season. We'd have known that, too, for no car could have survived it. The point is this: an incredible stag was living in an intensely farmed and hunted region and had not been detected. For all I knew, I was the only person who ever saw him up close.

The secret of the whitetail's success is simply his success at keeping secret. Given an option, he'll always play it sly.

I once started a whitetail buck near the head of a timbered valley. Flag up, he ran out of sight around a bend of the creek. I tracked him in the new snow. As soon as he was out of sight, he began walking slowly uphill, stopping now and then to look down his backtrail. At the top of the hill was a three-wire fence that the deer had crawled under. The bottom wire was just 17 inches from the ground. I measured it. To appreciate this, try crawling under a low fence with a small rocking chair strapped to your head. That buck did. He could have jumped that fence from a standing start. It would have been far easier, but it just wasn't the sly way to handle a fence with me coming up behind.

In manner of escape and evasion, the whitetail deer can be remarkably like the cottontail rabbit. (It's not unusual for deer to hide in big brushpiles in heavily hunted farm country.)

The cottontail starts with a burst of speed that quickly outdistances men and dogs. Then he slows or even stops and ambles around in a circle to his starting point, even though a couple of beagles may be singing down his trail. It's much the same with the cottontail deer—the flashy start and the sly circling back to home base.

Hunters long experienced in chasing deer with hounds report that such deer may not even run. At least not flat-out. Archibald Rutledge once said that in all his years of hunting he had seen only two or three deer in full flight before dogs, and in each case the deer was wounded and about to be caught. In front of hounds, Rutledge said, deer usually loaf along, dodge, make a few showy feints and spectacular jumps, but generally play it cool. He once watched a big buck at the head of a drive suddenly "appear like an apparition and then, with extraordinary skill, efface himself from the landscape." It was later found that the deer had turned and sneaked to safety between the hounds and the hunters.

I once played tag for four hours with a buck on a Mississippi River island. It was only about eight acres, but heavily covered. I was alone, hunting steadily and carefully, and I had one quick glimpse of the deer at the beginning and another just before I quit. So I knew that he hadn't left the island during the hunt. We were perfectly synchronized; if we hadn't been I might have killed him. But when I stopped, the deer stopped; when I sneaked, he sneaked. We must have cut each others' tracks a dozen times. By the end of the day I was kicking willows and saying things not for the young to hear. I came back the next day with Joe Martelle, my old river friend. You guessed it. The buck had left.

The whitetail's ability to adjust to man's doings is uncanny. A deer can even adjust to gunfire—if it's not being directed at him.

My son Chris and I were bowhunting one late October morning in the Glades, a wild tangle of Illinois River backwaters and bottomland not far from the Mississippi. We were on tree stands in big silver maples looking out over a cornfield that had been sharecropped.

There were local mallards and woodies back in the swamp, and duck blinds only a couple of hundred yards behind us. We hadn't counted on that. In the frosty dawn the big shotguns were thunderous. And yet, stealing down a cornrow toward us came a fat whitetail buck. At each salvo of the 12-bores back in the Glades, the buck lowered his head a notch and kept walking directly toward the guns. He was alert but not particularly nervous. He must have had a good reason. Probably trailing a doe. Anyway, it was clear that he knew the shooting wasn't at him, and when we last saw him he was still heading back into the swamp in the direction of the gunfire.

The whitetail is one of a kind, a big-game species that thrives in small-game habitats. No other large mammal could have done it; none has that unique set of qualities and responds so well to management. In most states today, this deer is the biggest and most prized of wildlife. It has special meaning to the ordinary hunter, not just as big game, but as available big game. It is the common man's chance for high personal adventure—and often his only chance.

There's all that, and something more.

Whitetails aren't often hunted in real wilderness. They are often hunted in the tamest of farmlands. But even in a horse-weed patch at the edge of a cornfield, a deer lends special wildness to the land so that wherever the deer is found it is a truly wild place. Deer carry wilderness entangled in their antlers; their hoofprints put the stamp of wildness on tame country.

When I was growing up in the mid-1930s, our part of central Iowa held a lot for an outdoor boy. But deer weren't part of it. About the only deer we had was a little fenced herd in the Ledges State Park on the Des Moines River. They were interesting, but they didn't offer much to small boys who loved to prowl the woods. They were park deer, kept deer. They were not real deer, if you see my meaning.

I was about 14 the time dad and I were fishing the Des Moines River, and I took a shortcut across the inside of a big sandbar. There was a dead buck lying there at the edge of the willows. There was no sign of injury. The buck was just dead, maybe four or five days dead, fly-blown and swollen. It was the first wild deer I had ever seen, dead or alive, and it instantly changed my world.

He was imposing. His rack, still with some tatters of dried velvet on them, seemed huge. I had never been so close to a deer. There was no fence around this one. He had been ranging free, leaving his great heart-shaped prints at muddy creek edges, and finally leaving his corporeal being here for a boy to find. Buzzards and possums would soon remove that, but something of the deer's presence would stay to renew the spirit that had faded from the valley 60 years before.

An almost tangible change had come over the sandbar—the thing that comes when a boy is touched by genuine wildness for the first time. It's something like falling in love. Windows had opened in my horizons, revealing wonders out back of beyond. Up until then I had played at imagining this valley to be a wild place, though I knew it wasn't. But to find a wild deer there!

That has been 40 years ago, and I still vividly remember the quality of light on the sand and the striped willow-shade that lay across the dead deer's flanks. There suddenly seemed to be a dusty quality to the light, and a hush and suspension of all moving things. It was the old spell of wildness that other boys have felt in all other times, and it must always be the same.

I dropped my fishing rod and tore off to fetch dad. He was as impressed as I. We must have hung around there for an hour or more, marveling and speculating and not knowing what to do about it. Dad told me all he knew about deer, which wasn't much, but it was impressive at the time. So was the sudden revelation that inside my stern, graying father there was a boy my own age. I suspected then, and know now, that men and boys are about the same when confronted with genuine wildness. It makes boys older somehow, and men younger, and they may come together at a common point on common ground.

I prize the whitetail as huntable game. There is none better. I prize his fine meat and soft leather, and I waste neither. But even more, I cherish the whitetail deer for breathing wildness into our bland, tame countrysides—reminding us of old times and old doings and the meaning of being young and free.

The Bum
Husband

THIS IS BEING WRITTEN ON VALENTINE'S DAY, when I often repent my flaws as a marital partner. By the time you've read it, my conscience will have scabbed over and I'll have backslid again.

Anyway, I often wonder how any normal woman can stand living with a sportsman. Hunting and fishing have done little to enhance my bride's domestic career, to say nothing of her social life. I bring home some of the raunchiest bums extant—cockle-burred tramps with three-day beards, mud to their eyeballs, and breaths freighted with strong drink. They disrupt the sleeping household, track up her floors, and teach her children to lie and use coarse language. By the time her son was twelve, he was already ruined for anything but flycasting, gunshooting and dog-running. She is haunted by the spectre that her three daughters may end up marrying such bums. And the way she says it, you know that she's less than half-joking.

But mostly I just come home alone, and that's bad enough.

My total overdue time adds up to about a third of our married life. The annual ammunition bill has often exceeded our annual fuel bill, and I spend my clothing budget on fishing tackle instead of shirts and then swipe shirt money out of the contingency fund. Before I owned a gun cabinet I kept my cased guns in the closet where they frequently fell, dragging a couple of her dresses to the floor where old Meanface Kelly—the world's worst Irish setter—might lie on them.

My wife always owns exactly what I need for my chores. Kitchen sponges were designed for cleaning and oiling boots. Fingernail lacquer is for touching up rod windings and fishing lures. Her household ammonia helps cut copper fouling from rifle barrels, and I used to find that cloth diapers were ideal for guncleaning patches. I use her scouring powder to shine up the bores of guns to be gyp-traded, and her talcum for powdering my right cheek for hot-weather trapshooting. Wet percale pillow cases are fine for carrying fish, and the bathtub is ideal for dipping bird dogs that are loaded with ticks and fleas, which is frequent.

When I refinish gunstocks in the basement, she can't do laundry because of the lint problem. And some years ago I test-fired a .38 handgun in the basement without warning her, causing her to drop a certain Haviland china platter. That was the year I cut up her soft leather yard shoes for slingshot pockets and kept a cageful of live rattlesnakes in the garage. And some frozen rattlesnake heads in the freezer, come to think of it. They were in there with a frozen owl.

Now and then she gets strident about the car, for it is washed only once in the summer and not quite that often in winter—unless one of the dogs has been sick in back—and there's little point in having the dents ironed out, trees and rocks being what they are.

Yet, she puts up with me, maybe because she knows she's my only Valentine. I couldn't chase another woman if I wanted to. Hunting and fishing keep me too broke, too tired, and too raunchy. Besides, my bird dog doesn't take kindly to other women and it's too late for either of us graying old pups to learn new tricks.

The Passing
of Little Sam

IT WAS A GOOD YEAR FOR RABBIT PRODUCTION. It's a good winter for hunting.

But the rabbits around home are safer this winter, and Saturday has lost its music. Little Sam is gone.

He was a scruffy, thicket-torn little beagle that owned my friend Big John Stetson. He was small enough to ride in Big John's hunting coat, but big enough to be boss.

That Little Sam was the smelliest dog we've ever known. Riding with him in a closed car when he was excited was enough to gag a maggot. He was the only dog that actually smelled better after fighting a skunk. Sam smelled every way that a dog can smell, and a few extra ways that he invented. But he smelled best with his nose, and that's what counted.

He was the slowest of all slow-trailers. A blind rabbit with the gout could outrun him. The older he got, the slower he got. That worked out fine, because a rabbit was never scared enough to hole up. Little Sam sort of lulled the rabbit into a sense of false security. He'd turn that rabbit easy-like, and sing him right back into your pocket.

On our last hunt together, we had twelve fine races with Sam, bagged a few rabbits and educated some others, and there wasn't a cottontail in the bunch that ever drew a deep breath. Being chased by Sam was a very restful occupation.

Little Sam trained at least three small boys. My Chris shot his first rabbits ahead of Sam, and so did Big John's oldest sons, Johnny and Jeff. Sam knew the rabbit, and he knew the boys, and he divided his heart between them.

Sam wandered off down the creek a while back. He was almost eleven years old, and ailing. We like to think that he was chasing one last rabbit, and he probably was, because not even the grim business of dying could have been more important to Sam than the happy business of rabbits. We wonder if that last rabbit sensed the honor that was being paid him.

Attaboy, Little Sam! Ho, Sam! Speak to him!

Pheasants Beyond Autumn

THERE IS A DICHOTOMY IN PHEASANT HUNTING, as in any hunting that is worth doing. There are sets of paired contrasts: two pheasant seasons, two kinds of hunters, two types of birds. Gold and gray, gay and grim, yin and yang.

One pheasant season may last no longer than opening weekend—a brief, burnished time with Indian summer still on the land, the afternoons soft and tawny and hunters with their coats open. The other pheasant season is quieter and grayer, reaching far into December. The sky is often stone-colored then, filled with prairie winds that cut with a wire edge, and even on clear days the sunlight is pale and without substance.

In that first pheasant season there were hunters by the hundreds of thousands, sweeping the fields in wide lines with deployed blockers, plaguing farmers and each other, shooting at pheasants hopelessly far away, ripping out the crotches of new hunting pants on bobwire fences, and generally having a helluva time. They head back to town with or without birds, often making a stop along the way and arriving home late and smelling like hot mince pies. They are not likely to reappear on the landscape for about one year.

The pheasant hunters who do return, and keep returning, have a singular worn quality. Their canvas coats are likely to be weatherstained and shapeless, with the main button missing and a pronounced sag in the region of the game pocket, and their gunmetal is worn to the white. They hunt without haste—dour men in twos and threes, or often alone with an old retriever at heel. Men shaped and colored by circumstance, as fitted to their environment as horseweeds and cockleburs—and just as enduring and tenacious. They must be, to match the birds that they now hunt.

The pheasants of the opening weekend were overwhelmingly birds of the year, callow juveniles that rose clattering into the air within easy gun range. Those birds went home with the opening-day hunters and, like them, will not reappear for another year. The birds that remain are either sagacious old roosters with long spurs, or smart young cocks that won their spurs during the first week of hunting. Such pheasants have much in common with the remaining hunters. Each tempers and hones the other in a process of mutual refinement.

There is some loss of pheasants with the first intense shock of cold weather. There is a marked loss of hunters as well. By then, both pheasant and hunter have evolved beyond their opening-day counterparts—for it needs a tougher breed of hunter to pit himself against the pheasant range of late December, and a tougher breed of pheasant to resist him. But somehow, the pheasant tends to harden and sharpen a bit ahead of the man who hunts him, even the very good man. There comes a point where hunter persistence is outstripped by pheasant resistance—and the roosters always win.

The December pheasant is the real pheasant and to hunt him is to hunt pheasants truly. Which is not to say that opening weekend is unworthy of serious regard. It is a very special time, a season apart, that late October or early November opening. A wedding party and honeymoon in one—green and golden preface to a hardworking marriage between bird and gunner.

Opening Day is when a small boy is allowed to tag along for

the first time and maybe even carry dad's first rooster of the day, and get to keep the tail feathers. The boy will soon be carrying a 20-bore and a rooster of his own.

It is a time when the clans gather, when old hunting pards rendezvous. They come from all compass points, reaffirming the faith. I'll go home to central Iowa again and hook up with Harry Harrison or Skeeter Wheeler. Or Glen Yates—leathery, irascible, ornery, deeply regarded Yates. Sly old cuss Yates, with his bib overalls and tattered coat and Sweet Sixteen, and a profound and abiding knowledge of the ring-necked pheasant. Opening Day is playday for us. It's Gooney Bird Day, time to test the young roosters and see how all the folks are doing out there in the fields. As Yates puts it: "Of course Opening Day ain't pheasant hunting. Hell, that ain't new. But it's the start of it— and Kee-rist, Madseen, am I ready!"

It's this Opening Day that largely supports wildlife conservation in much of the Midwest—notably Iowa, Kansas, Nebraska and South Dakota. License sales soar just before the pheasant season, swelling the game and fish coffers while gun and ammunition receipts build the Pittmann-Robertson fund. In Iowa, about 300,000 residents buy hunting licenses. About 290,000 of them hunt pheasants—and probably 80 percent are out there on the great Saturday. If there were no pheasant opening in Iowa, as many as 200,000 licenses might go unsold in a given year— and the wildlife conservation program would go down the tube. It is much the same elsewhere. Let us look kindly on Opening Day.

A lot of bird hunting isn't really hunting. For example, you don't hunt waterfowl and wild turkey. You seduce and delude them. Nor do men usually hunt quail. They hunt for the dog that's hunting for the quail.

Early-season pheasant hunting isn't as likely to be hunting so much as just combing through cover. Birds are likely to be almost anywhere in the early November fields and edges, so it's usually a matter of just pointing yourself at the general landscape and grinding out mileage.

But later pheasant hunting may be as pure a form of hunting

as there is. The hunter then becomes a classic searcher and stalker, shooting less and hunting much, much more. There are still a few ribbon clerks trying to shoot pheasants from cars— but that's a pallid imitation of sport that doesn't really produce much. While the pheasant season is still young, the birds have begun to shrink away from roadsides. The slow ones are dead, and most of the others are likely to be somewhere back in the fields where things are more peaceful. (With exceptions, of course. We know a man who hunts late-season birds in the thick brome of certain I-80 interchanges. He says he does all right. As near as we can figure it, the only law he's breaking is the one prohibiting pedestrians on interstate highways.)

I don't have much late-season cunning, but one practice that's worked out well is simply getting as far as possible from roads. An obvious reason is that most birds have faded away from roadside field edges. Then, too, the very center of a square-mile section of midwestern cornland may be the untidiest part. It's where a farmer tends to sweep stuff under the rug, back where passersby can't see small farm dumps, weed patches, messy fencerows and junk machinery.

I once found a mile-square section whose exact center was low and boggy, and whose owner had never gone to the expense and effort of extending tile lines from there to the nearest road ditch a half-mile away. Since the swale was probably lower than the distant road ditch, drainage wouldn't have been possible, anyway. The result was a little two-acre oasis that was abandoned to wild grasses and forbs. And pheasants, of course. Unless a man stood on the cab of his pickup truck (which I did), this could not be seen from the road.

In contrast is a certain square mile of central Iowa farmland that lies on a terminal moraine. In most of my home country a man can plow all day and not see a stone bigger than a walnut, but this particular township has sprinklings of glacial erratics. Over the years, farmers had removed such debris from their fields to a slight lift of land in the center of my hunting ground, where today a modest boulderfield covers almost an acre— together with several rolls of old fencing and a mantle of gold-

enrod, lesser ragweed, and sumac. This little niche is a magnet
for wildlife, although I never hit it hard nor often. Once a season
is enough.

Out here in the corn country—and about everywhere else—a
man must exploit two extremes in his late-season pheasant
hunting. He must hunt close and far, alternating between dense
coverts and wide, naked fields.

There are genuine pheasant hunters who think nothing of
reducing new canvas pants to shredded rags in the course of a
single hunting season. They churn around in terrible places—
deep pockets of raspberry canes undergrown with dense grass,
rough weedy creekbanks thick with catbriar tangles, and the
steep banks of old bullditches with their overgrowth of ragweed
and sumac. You know—the kinds of cover that hurt just to look
at. But these are the haunts of late-season roosters, and the men
who rout them out of such stuff do so with the premise that the
only places worth hunting in late season are in cover that no
sane man would ever enter.

Such attention to detail, and willingness to suffer for it,
applies to open field gunning as well. It may mean hunting in
rough plowing, such as plowed pastures where broken sod is left
to mellow over the winter. These are the devil's own fields to
walk in; the black surfaces of the upturned sods become as
slippery as grease during the midday thaw, and a man can break
his bones there. Still, roosters may be sheltering in sun-warmed
hollows between and under the big clods, and a hunter must go
where the birds may be. If there's any comfort in this, it's
knowing that pheasants are as reluctant to run in heavy plowing
as men are. Well, almost.

This breed of hunter will turn aside from a comfortable fence-
line and stumble across a quarter of plowing to hunt a wisp of
grassed waterway only a few yards long, or walk hundreds of
yards out of his way to investigate a basket-sized tuft of foxtail
in a picked cornfield, or a distant hay bale that the farmer failed
to pick up. No cover feature in the barren winter landscape is
too minor to overlook. It is hunting based on three articles of
faith: 1) that much of the pre-season rooster population is still

out there, and although 2) there is no cheap late-season pheasant, 3) the longer you hunt without flushing a bird, the closer
you are to flushing one.

Pheasants range more widely in winter than at any other time
of year. They are constantly adjusting to impending storms,
snow-choked roosts, and deep cold and wind. Vagaries of wind
and snow drifting will eliminate certain niches of the birds'
range, and bring others into play. Marvelously rugged and
adaptable birds, winter pheasants never cease probing and
exploring.

Aldo Leopold observed that Wisconsin pheasants were sometimes restless in coverts of less than ten acres. Where small
coverts prevailed, pheasants were likely to adopt a winter "cir-
cuit-type" movement, traveling from one covert to another in a
sequence spreading over a mile of distance and several days'
time. Leopold believed that Wisconsin pheasants in good winter
range had an average cruising radius of one-eighth to one-half
mile, and two or three miles at the most.

Since today's winter coverts in the primary pheasant range are
almost always less than ten acres, such fiddle-footed drifting
may be a common trait in many regions. Although a particular
covert may not hold birds today, it doesn't mean that they might
not be there tomorrow or a couple of days from now. On the
contrary, it could mean that they probably will be.

Our most successful wild birds and mammals are those that
have not been fixed in rigid frames of specialization, but are
generalized in design and function. The pheasant is a pretty
good example of this, owing much of his success to a rather
generalized form and a knack for ready adjustment. We can't
really ascribe much intelligence to the pheasant. After all, the
chicken tribe wasn't at the head of the line when the brains were
passed out. But the ringneck is certainly "country smart;" he
may not know his way to town, but he sure ain't lost. He
develops a remarkably shrewd sense of range. Not as well as the
red fox or whitetail deer, perhaps, but infinitely better than the
men who hunt him there.

We human hunters are likely to regard countrysides in terms

of drainage systems and patterns of cultivation and habitation. Or, at best, in terms of entire brushy creeks, dry sloughs and weedy fields. Wild hunted creatures like the pheasant learn their native heath in terms of minute, intimate crannies—little sections of overhung creekbank, the tree stump covered with vines and weeds, that old roll of fencewire smothered with giant foxtail. Our eyes are always about six feet above the ground; the pheasant's are down there among the details, down in the tangled heart of the covert, and an instant later his eyes may be 40 feet in the air. A pheasant is exposed to the major and minor features of his home range in ways that the hunter can never hope to be, and he is highly capable of exploiting that exposure in stress situations.

While trading from one major winter covert to another, a pheasant is about as likely to walk as fly. In the course of such commuting he continually adds to his experience bank. If the obvious winter hangouts are regularly disturbed by hunters, many ringnecks begin to rely on interim coverts—little pockets of sanctuary that they have happened upon along the way. This occurs too often to be a fluke—occasions when certain birds are not to be found in any conventional shelter-belt or weedy slough, but are shut down in the weedy mouth of an old culvert or in a snug form of tented bluegrass in an orchard. The compleat pheasant hunter must learn to think in such terms. This is one of the reasons that I enjoy hunting pheasant on snow. It's all written out there, although I often fail to comprehend what I read.

It's on snow that one can trace daily feeding patterns, some of the winter circuitry between far-flung coverts, and the bewildering and often admirable interactions of winter pheasants and their harsh world. Such tracking is more likely to instruct in natural history than to result in shooting. My lifetime success rate for converting pheasant tracks to Sunday dinners can't be much more than two percent. Something usually goes wrong.

But if I've learned one thing about trailing, it's this: to never think in terms of a pheasant resting placidly at the end of a line of tracks. If those tracks are really fresh, the pheasant is almost certainly aware of being trailed and you will rarely get a shot while the bird is on the move. It's his pausing-place that you must find. If the trail appears to lead across rather open ground to a distant pocket of weedy cover, swing far to the side and come in from behind. I think this may be the only way I've ever trailed and killed pheasants—by leaving the trail and flanking the bird at some point ahead. Several times, on fresh snow, I have found that roosters had entered bits of cover and had hooked around in order to watch their backtrails.

Snow lends certain advantages to the pheasant hunter. Birds can be more easily seen in distant feeder fields and coverts in snowtime, crippled birds can be readily trailed, and dead pheasants are easier to find in heavy cover. Yet, snowtime is hardly a situation in which the calloused gunner exploits a vulnerable population and kills pheasants at will. My success rate at tracking and shooting pheasants on snow is about the same as my fox-trailing with a rifle—reinforcing my long-held conviction that the ring-necked pheasant is nothing less than a feathered fox.

There's something I miss in my late-season hunting these days.

For years I have begun pheasant hunts on wheels instead of legs, leaving home in car or truck, driving as many miles as necessary, and returning in comfort. The day that I began to do this marked the end of my boyhood and pushed back the prairie horizons, but it wasn't necessarily progress.

It will never be like just stepping off the back stoop and loading my gun, walking across the garden, and being in hunting grounds almost at once. Pure hunting, that was, from home den out into the coverts and back to den again, like a young fox. It was never diluted, as now, with synthetic beginnings on highways.

Each cover patch would point to one beyond until I had overextended myself as I always did, and night had found me far from home. There is a keen and poignant quality in being a famished boy far afield with night coming on and miles of crusted snow yet to negotiate, the pheasants hanging over your shoulder with their legs tied with binder twine, and the little

Monkey Ward double gun beginning to weigh heavy. (I had bought the gun's mismatched 16-gauge shells at Walsh's Hardware, out of a bin where they were all mixed together and served up like rock candy—three cents apiece and you took what came up in the scoop, with no picking over the shells for preferred shot sizes or other such nonsense.)

Night coming on and glory lost, for there would be no daylight in which to parade past neighbor girls' houses, the bright roosters hung from my shoulder. The girls would never know what they had missed, but I would.

Now, for the first time in ten hours, a weakness beginning in the legs, and that exquisite knifelike stab high between the shoulder blades. Ten hours since oatmeal and coffee, with long crossings over plowed ground, and ranging through horseweed thickets laced with wild plum and raspberry canes, through fallow pastures of heavy tented grass, creekside willow slaps, over the high fields and under the bluffs, and into little cattail sloughs whose icy floors were skeined with pheasant tracks. And once, a half-mile dash along a crusted fenceline trying to flush a running rooster and failing to, gasping in the cold air and coughing for an hour afterward.

My lips and nose would be raw and sore from hours of wiping them with the backs of woolen mittens that were quickly frozen. There was a winter twilight when I stopped and leaned against an old wolf cottonwood to rest, and took off my woolen stocking cap to mop my sore nose. It was the first time since morning that I'd taken off the cap; when I ran my fingers through my matted hair it protested at being disturbed, and I remember thinking it was funny that even my hair should hurt, but not funny enough to laugh about.

The wind freshening, swinging into the northwest and freighted with the smell of more snow. By now my corduroy pants are frozen to the knees, as stiff as stovepipes and rattling against each other and against the shoepacs that I had bought with my first fur check the year before. One foot ahead of the other, breaking through snow crust at each step, the slung birds cutting through old sheepskin coat and into thin shoulder, and a sort of homesickness growing at the sight of each lighted kitchen window in farmhouses across the fields. And finally, up ahead in the gathering darkness, a square of yellow reflecting on snow, strangely warm and vivid after the long hours of unrelieved white and gray. There ahead, a circle of light and warmth for a young hunter come home of a winter evening, late in pheasant season.

At last, up the back steps and out of the wild night into the rich kitchen smell of home, where potroast with whole onions and carrots and potatoes is waiting on the back of the stove, and buttercrusted rolls still hot, with much-loved voices laughing and half-scolding and the close comfort of it wrapping a boy like a grandmother's quilt. I would take off coat and mittens before I began eating—but only because mother forced me to. And soon to sleep, out in the back room with its icy linoleum, mounded over with lamb's-wool comforters and fleecy blankets smelling of cedar, the deep guiltless slumber of a hunter who has spent everything that he had of himself, and hunted as well as he knew how.

Just being young was part of this, of course, and coming home was part of it, too. But there was more—a wild purity of hunting that was wholly free and true. It was hunting with all the fat rendered away, and reduced to the clean white bone. It was a closing of the magic circle of man, animal and land, and once a boy glimpses this he remembers it all of his days.

This is the essence for which I will always hunt, for I often misplace it and seem seldom able to find it in the old full measure that I knew. But when it's found, it will likely be on some iron prairie at the knell of the year, with a cunning old ringneck out ahead and showing me the way.

Part II

UNDER THE SUN,
BY THE SIDE OF THE WIND

What would the world be, once bereft
Of wet and of wildness? Let them be left,
O let them be left, wildness and wet;
Long live the weeds and the wilderness yet.

Gerard Manley Hopkins

Message from
a Desert Island

HORN ISLAND. As desert islands go, this place is just right. It hangs out here in the blue Gulf thirteen miles off Biloxi—far enough from the mainland to discourage Sunday boaters but close enough to float rum bottles with messages back to the coast. Few Yankees know the island is here. Most mainlanders do, but leave it alone. No one lives here. The little island is left pretty much to itself, raked by Gulf squalls and warmed by Gulf sun, the sea eagles nesting above the snowy beaches and the gators bellowing in the swamps.

Old Sieur de Bienville named it, they say, when one of his men lost a powder horn here. For most of the time since 1699 it has been simply Horn Island—one of the chain of little barrier islands strung along our coast with its neighbors, Petit Bois, Dauphin, Ship and Cat islands.

Horn is a new part of our Gulf Islands National Seashore, a reasonable sort of desert island that doesn't carry things to extremes—it has enough trees to break the blinding glare of the sand, and a couple of little springs that keep us hydrated. Yet, it meets all the requirements of a proper desert island—total solitude, trackless beaches and buried gold. We haven't done anything about the gold yet; we're diverted by more practical treasures.

We found one of those treasures yesterday.

When the research boat *Sea Squirt* marooned us here we had ample provisions. But some staples are running low, and for the past four days we've been trying to find the source of those oyster shells that litter the beach. My wife Dycie and son Chris found a few oysters in the sea, but the mother lode eluded us. And in our scale of immediate values, fresh oysters are more useful than old gold.

Yesterday morning I wandered over some high beach dunes and down to a little salt creek. There were some empty oyster shells among the rushes, so I waded out. Near the shore, in no more than two feet of water, I struck it rich. In a few minutes I filled a small seabag with oysters and swaggered back up the beach. Behold the provider! Dycie and Chris and I sat at the edge of the gentle surf and ate fat oysters as fast as we could shuck them. We aren't very good at this oyster shucking yet, but love conquereth all.

We returned with the avowed intention of eating our way through fifty yards of oyster bed. We'll never make it. We slosh when we walk, wearing idiot grins of satisfaction. Tonight Dycie is taking the lantern out onto the flats again, to spear flounder. Our bully beef is gone, but who cares?

It's been said that Horn Island was once part of the mainland, and that the intervening land sank below sea level to form offshore islands. But today it's known that Horn and its sister islands were built by ancient hurricanes, perhaps 6,000 years ago.

A barrier island like Horn can be formed as an "equilibrium structure" on a shallow, shelving coast at some point where wave attack is balanced by bottom resistance. When seas run high and wild under a giant hurricane, a pre-existing submarine sandbar is built up until it bears the same relationship to the level of the storm sea that it had to normal sea levels. When the storm seas subside, a greatly elevated sandbar emerges as a long, narrow island. Today, Horn Island is about twelve miles long and nearly a mile wide in one place, tapering on each end to flat, sandy spits.

Horn Island was born of hurricanes, and is still shaped by them. Barrier islands are never static—each great storm changes them in some manner. The hurricane of 1960 shortened Horn Island a half-mile on its eastern end and lengthened it a quarter-mile on the west.

The onslaught of hurricanes on these exposed little islands must be incredible. The great storm seas may sweep entirely over the islands, smashing and drowning, impelling trees like pile drivers, tearing away the dunes and the life that exists on them.

We've heard of only one man who survived a Horn Island hurricane. He was Walter I. Anderson of Ocean Springs, Mississippi, a naturalist and artist who often rowed his small boat out to Horn and camped there for weeks at a time, working and dreaming. He always wondered what a Horn Island hurricane was like, and in 1965 he found out.

Hurricane Betsy struck in September that year, with torrents of rain and winds up to ninety miles per hour. Anderson was camping alone on Horn when the wall of wind and sea struck the island. As the water rose to his armpits, he tied the painter of his little boat around his waist and headed for the highest sand dune he could reach. He spent a night and the following day in the shelter of the dune, bludgeoned by wind and rain, and saw his favorite wild pig washed away.

He was luckier than the lighthouse keeper of Horn Island, who tried to brave the hurricane of 1906. Lightkeeper Nelson had been warned by the best fisherman on that part of the coast, who stopped by Horn in his dash for safety. But the lightkeeper elected to stay despite the warning, and the hurricane swept away the lighthouse, killing Nelson, his wife, and daughter.

The barrier islands have a grim storm history that dates back to 1717, but all storms fade before 1969's Camille—the most powerful hurricane that ever struck a populated coastline. Weather planes clocked Camille's winds at 218 mph, and recorded the lowest barometric pressure ever read: 26.01 inches of mercury. Ship Island was cut into three pieces by that storm, and over a third of its vegetation was ripped away. Large live oaks on Cat Island were uprooted, and groves of slash pines leveled. The raging seas swept over much of Horn Island, washing away 8,700 feet of its western end and about 1,800 feet of the eastern end of the island. Mainland beaches were strewn with dead wildlife washed into Mississippi Sound from the islands. Yet, Horn Island still had birds after Camille had passed, and there were fresh pig tracks. In our prowlings around this island, Chris and I haven't noted any great damage to Horn's live oaks and slash pines. Tall pines stand as staunch as ever—some are more than two hundred years old, veterans of many hurricanes before Camille.

There are countless smaller storms—such as the equinoctial squalls of late March and late September. We went through one of those the other night.

A brisk wind had blown all day, and as it freshened in late afternoon we moved camp from the north beach and set up behind the main dunes. By half past five we could see a low black wall coming out of the west, and the storm struck at six o'clock. We had eaten earlier than usual so that we could secure the camp, driving four-foot stakes deep into the sand and replacing our tents' beckets with short lengths of shock cord. It was about then that we noticed that the shrimp boat anchored in the sound off the north beach had left—heading for the sheltered anchorage at Pascagoula.

Only our tough little mountain tents could have weathered it. A wall tent would have carried away at the first blast. The wind sent sand streaming from the crests of the dunes like blowing snow; it is always strange, seeing that but not feeling cold. The rain drove horizontally into the camp, and we dressed in oilskins to watch the show, standing on the dunes in a strange coral-colored light that tinted the sand. It was well that we had moved up off the beach; our old campsite now had seas running across it.

The front had passed by eight o'clock, and the little camp still stood. In fact, like the house that Pooh built for Eeyore, it was even improved a little. A clear, quiet night came on, washed clean and filled with stars. We built our night fire, and Dycie's wonderful coffee ("I brew the best pot on this island!") was even finer than usual. We drank it all.

As Gulf storms go, this wasn't much. The people on the mainland may have remarked on the rain beating against their picture windows, and then returned unruffled to evening television. It was a thing of no consequence. But out here on Horn, where great weathers are free to run unbridled and home is a scrap of taut nylon, even a little storm captures our full and undivided attention.

Something stirred up our neighbors this morning, and they were screaming all over the place. It wasn't our doing—we keep away from them and mind our own affairs, but it doesn't take much to upset nesting ospreys.

Our neighbors' nest is about four hundred yards from camp, bulking large in the top of a tall slash pine. We avoid the place, having learned early that the expectant couple throws a yelling fit if we come within a few hundred feet of their pine. We keep our distance; good fences make good neighbors, and so do four hundred yards.

We've never seen such an osprey population; this is what parts of the mainland must have looked like in the old days, before drainage, lumbering, and DDT. There is a big grove of pines on the other side of the island where Chris and I counted six nests on only a few hundred acres, with five ospreys aloft at one time. This is prime country for the fish hawks; the Gulf side of Horn Island is the first solid land this side of Yucatán, and its shoals must offer fine fishing. On Horn's north side—fronting Mississippi Sound—dilution by freshwater may affect some marine fish, making them more vulnerable to ospreys. Just a guess. I'm not sure about that, but the ospreys seem to be.

We've missed the waterfowl that wintered in the Horn Island

lagoons—the redheads, bluebills, canvasbacks, and others. It's late March now, and we have passed each other somewhere back up the line. We must have missed most of the plovers, too, but we're seeing a few king rails and clappers down in the marshes.

Dr. Don Bradburn, over in New Orleans, says that Horn is the western limit of the gray kingbird. Doc should know; he's an old Horn Island wanderer. We haven't seen those kingbirds, but they're around. So are some of the longrange migrants; we saw several bobolinks a few days ago, on their way north from Cuba or South America. We may see the same birds again, a thousand miles north of here, on our Iowa prairies. Several times, during long, hot hikes down the island, we have loafed in the shade of live-oak thickets and been serenaded by mockingbirds that seemed hungry for a human audience. All mockingbirds are hams, of course, but these outdo themselves.

Every time we walk across the island to the south beaches we see new rootings by wild pigs. Their tracks are everywhere in some places, but so far we haven't seen the pigs themselves. We think about them, however; our shrimp fisherman came ashore the other day to stretch his legs, and told us of once being treed when he surprised a wild sow with a litter of piglets. A more immediate concern is the possibility of a raid on the camp while we're gone. Whenever we leave, we secure camp and latch our heavy chop box. It might not stop a hungry hog, but it makes us feel better. However, they may see people so seldom that they are shy of us. And that, as Chris says, "ain't no bad thing."

We miss our canoes; they would be the best way to prowl around in the swamps on Horn and check on some of the alligators that we know are there, and maybe even see a river otter. Maybe next time.

Snakes are on my mind. Normally, I coexist happily with poisonous snakes and hardly give them a thought—beyond agreeing with their taste for rough country. But we're out here with no boat, no radio, no antivenin, and there are cottonmouths and copperheads. When we wade after oysters we keep an eye out for cottonmouths, and when walking in the groves we stay on clear, open ground. We keep special watch on Little Jo, for she's built very close to the ground and her five years haven't taught her much about vipers. But, like the wild hogs, the poisonous snakes are not manifest.

The old records don't indicate that wildlife ever abounded on Horn Island, although there may always have been plenty of gators and water moccasins. The most common wildlife is birds, and 178 species have been reported on Horn. There are apparently no deer here; there may never have been. The biggest mammals are the wild pigs, raccoons, nutria, and possibly otters, and we've had glimpses of cottontails and swamp rabbits. Hurricanes surely scourge the mammal populations, but they recover in one way or another. Walter Anderson often saw small mammals clinging to floating debris in the sound, drifting toward the islands and an eventual restocking.

Our spring bubbles out of a sand dune near a clump of tough beach shrubbery. It flows about ten gallons per hour, and the little stream fans out in the sand and vanishes in a few yards. It's not easy to find—but the residents know where it is. There are always signs of small comings and goings—mice, rats, rabbits, and other minor critters. We drink by day, they by night, and the spring never wants for customers.

There's no walking down the center of Horn Island. The center ranges from marshy to marshier, and there are only a few places high enough to permit crossing the island from north to south. So our main travel routes are down the great beaches, with short detours back into the woods and marsh edges.

We've walked fourteen miles of south beach without seeing any footprints but our own. In places the main beach is a quarter-mile wide, lifting abruptly into a jumble of white dunes, some nearly fifty feet high, crowned with palmetto and rosemary. Just behind them are the first slash pines and live oaks, some partly buried in the dunes, and beyond that are the dark sedges and open ponds. The dunes facing the open sea take a savage mauling from storms, but some of them wear a mantle of sea oats, rosemary, groundsel, and wax myrtle, and that helps.

This south beach is a fascinating litter, courtesy of Camille. Driftwood, planks, shattered fragments of buildings, tree trunks, and bits of ship wreckage—including a rusty boiler from some large wreck. There is a profusion of both gin bottles and light bulbs; the Gulf's mariners, it appears, do not care to drink in the dark. Most of this junk is cast far up on the second beach; lower down, the sand lies pristine and trackless.

It's odd, the way a wild beach can draw us away from each other for a time, marooning each of us alone with his own thoughts. We can cross the island in a bunch—Dycie and I, Chris, Miss Leslie, and Little Jo—skylarking and chattering, to burst out of the pines and down to the beach in an excited rush. But once there, the haste and noise drop away, and wind and sea take us over. Soon we are absorbed in various matters, each drifting off on a course of his own, puttering alone without knowing it, or caring.

I find bittersweet pleasure in pausing far down some wild beach and turning to watch the family strung off through the distance—only dots, but each dot of vast significance. It is seeing happiness in a far perspective, and I savor such times, knowing that I can conjure up this picture sharp and clear long after most of the other pictures have blurred.

And then, after a couple of hours, the ineffable excitement of reunion, of coalescing as a family again, each with his own piece of news. Inevitably, one news item transcends the others—such as Leslie's discovery of a perfect flat of smooth white sand. It was as clean and featureless as a field of new snow. Inspired by its blankness, we organized a game of fox and geese, and the five of us whooped and churned around the big circle and along its spokes in what may have been the first game of fox and geese ever played on the Gulf of Mexico. It was a good workout, running in that loose sand. I carried Little Jo back to camp on my shoulder, and we sang all the way.

About that buried gold.

Late in the Civil War, with the United States drowning in its own blood, Napoleon III of France felt it was safe to violate our

Monroe Doctrine and seize the Mexican government. He placed the Archduke Maximilian von Hapsburg and the Archduchess Carlota on the Mexican throne, backing them with French troops. Maximilian was the first New World emperor since Montezuma, but his reign lasted only three years. The Civil War ended, and the United States bent an angry gaze toward Mexico. We officially supported Juárez in his popular revolution, and Napoleon III prudently withdrew support of Maximilian.

With the Mexican throne in jeopardy, the empress set out for France in 1866 to plead with Napoleon III for renewed support. She sailed from Veracruz acompanied by a field marshal, General Juan Almonte, and a treasure in French gold that Maximilian wanted desperately to keep out of Juárez' hands.

Their voyage had hardly begun when the ship was wrecked off the shore of Horn Island. Before it sank, the treasure was saved and secretly buried by General Almonte on Horn Island near a place called "The Alligator Swamp." Carlota, Almonte, and their officers and crew were shortly rescued by another French ship and returned to France. But Carlota's pleas to Napoleon III were unavailing; he refused to support Maximilian, who was soon overthrown and executed. Carlota broke under her grief and despair and became insane. General Almonte died in 1869. The only people who knew the treasure's location never returned to it, and there is no record of the gold ever being recovered. So somewhere in Horn Island's swampy heart lies a golden fortune. Oh, there's no doubt about it. Ask anyone.

Later, there was another treasure.

In March 1914 a Biloxi lad named Ben Bailey found five pounds of ambergris on the Horn Island beach. Formed in the intestines of unhappy sperm whales that have difficulty digesting the hard parts of giant squids, the gray, waxy, stinking stuff is invaluable as a fixative for fine perfumes. In 1914 it was worth about as much as gold—$35 per ounce—and young Bailey's find was valued at almost $3,000. There was one person, though, who didn't join in the general rejoicing. Mrs. William Waters, who lived on Horn Island, had found ten pounds of the ambergris before Ben Bailey found his—and she had destroyed it to keep her dogs from wallowing in it. To her dying day, Mrs. Waters must have kicked every sweet-smelling dog she met.

Gold and ambergris are enough to put a craving on any beachcomber. But at the moment, as noted earlier, we are occupied with more practical treasures.

I'm scribbling the last of this under the bush by the spring, which is my principal place, and I've just heard a hail from Dycie and the kids down on the beach. Our shrimper is in from his night's work and has put ashore in his dinghy. They're all talking. Shrimper is lifting a tub from the dinghy. Now they're jumping up and down. Translation: a tubful of shrimp or blue crabs or oysters, or maybe all three.

Must go. Will be in touch.

Requiem
for a Small River

WE GREW UP ON THE BEST PART OF THE RIVER, where the North Fork of the Skunk, also called the Cha-Ca-Gua, began to break out of the terminal moraine of the last glacial advance into central Iowa.

The little river had a good gradient there, and as prairie streams go, it went pretty good. Down a rather narrow valley, flanked with low ridges of bur oak and pasture, the Skunk sauntered along through groves of ash, elm, and cottonwood—as unhurried and independent as its namesake.

There were a few places, our favorites, where it flowed beside limestone ledges fed from deep springs, or over sheets of bedrock used as wagon fords. It slid past loam cutbanks and clay cliffs where it dug holes almost as deep as the river was wide, under log drifts where big catfish lay, across flats of bright sand with their schools of redhorse suckers, and then ran off down sloping floors of glacial pebbles, ankle-deep and laughing. On the inside of each deep bend was a sandbar—and to country boys, deep water shoaling into sand can mean only one thing.

For three months of the year those sandbars were peopled with small boys—naked, raucous, undisciplined, and wonderfully free boys with sun-bleached hair and skins burned dark except where overall straps crossed their shoulders. We had Barebutt Beach #1 at Maxwell's Bend; up near Olsen's Farm was Barebutt #2. I was always partial to #1, myself. It was near a melon patch.

South of there a few miles the valley widened as the Skunk entered a much older bed. In times past, that broader valley had been an impassable bog of quicksand and prairie sloughs. Tile drains solved the slough problem, but there were still those June floods when the river came swelling up out of its channel and over the floodplain to reclaim its own.

That part of the Skunk was channelized and tamed before I was born, which is getting to be a few years, now.

Draglines had cut a long, straight channel and deepened it; spoil was heaped high on the banks for levees. Bends, deep holes, riffles, sandbars, log drifts—all normal river features vanished. The channel was now deep and straight, and high water sped down it like a sluiceway. The river lost its identity as a river, and no longer held interest for man, boy, or fish. I cannot recall anyone ever condemning that barren stretch of river or the process that made it what it was—it simply did not exist for us. No one trapped, fished, or swam there. It was tacitly regarded as the lower limit of the real river, as if the Skunk had suddenly drained into a blankness.

And so we grew up with the images of two rivers in our heads. One was as vivid and real and young as we were. The lower river was a ghost. No, it was less than that, for a ghost would have held some interest for us. It was just a place that had stopped being. A rural gutter, as functional as any other and just as drab. I can still recall my intense surprise years later, as a budding limnologist, when I learned of an old record of muskellunge in the river before it had been gutterized. Only then did I have an inkling of what had been lost.

Now a lake is a fine place with much to offer, but there is a certain sadness in it, too, for it is a prisoner that must lie helpless in its basin as the invading land slowly chokes and buries it. From the moment a lake is born, it begins to die. Not so with a river. From the moment a river is born it begins to grow and travel, working and moving on, changing the land and giving it the features that make country worth living in.

I know many wild lakes that are splendid places—no doubt of that. But to me, they aren't a patch on the rivers that feed and drain them. That's where the action is—the life, the movement and changing. I'd infinitely rather fish or canoe in a stream than a lake. Which isn't to say that I do not respect lakes. But while an engineer may build a lake that's a fair imitation of the real thing, you'll never see anyone building a good stream.

There are many kinds of good streams. Any stream is good if it's allowed to keep some of its integrity. It needn't be a snow-fed mountain creek with waterfalls and all. It can be a big, brown river like the Missouri or Mississippi, a mature river, solid and strong, wandering through a broad floodplain that it began carving eons ago. A grandfather river. I like to go out and set hoopnets and basket traps, snooping around such backwaters as Jug Handle Slough and the Butterfly Chute and the Stump Patch, poling through green caverns out into vast beds of lotus, heavy with fragrance and ablaze with sunlight.

I also like to ride on the little limestone rivers of the Ozarks— rivers that may be almost as old as the Mississippi but which have kept their youth. Bright, laughing streams, moving over their gravel beds and drowned ledges, fed by watercressed springs from under towering walls. The Mississippi and our other senior rivers are very solemn, and take themselves very seriously. Little limestone rivers are never solemn. They move with soft laughter and subtle music; they dance with your canoe, teasing it and running lightly beside it, cool and sweet, with the caprice and innocence of Indian girls.

Some of the best streams of all are the small farmland rivers. Modest places, rarely spectacular, but lending a measure of freedom and wildness to landscapes that are thoroughly plowed, cowed, and put to cash grain. In many parts of our Midwest, South and Southeast—rich humid regions that are intensely

cultivated—such streams are among the best escape routes from
the soul-bruising press of modern living.

The best of these are bordered with greenbelts of timber that
persist because the shoulders of the river valley are too steep to
farm, or the floodplains are too subject to overflow. It is possible
to float for days with walls of forest slipping past on each side,
and a sandbar at every bend for your evening camp. The farms
just beyond the trees are forgotten, and the highway bridges
quickly left behind. There are purists who demean such experience as only an illusion of real wilderness and freedom—but
they're wrong. Wilderness and freedom, like any other types of
beauty, are relative qualities. Someday, maybe, you and I will
really canoe the Coppermine or Mackenzie and go adventuring
into regions "where nameless men by nameless rivers wander."
And maybe we won't. Until then, let no one demean our mini-
adventures on the rivers of home, for even a mini-adventure
assumes remarkable proportions when compared with the steril-
ity of television and air-conditioned suburbs.

Then there are the least of our rivers—the little farm creeks
that poke along through woodlots and pastures, replete with a
few somnolent cows, punkinseed sunfish, feisty dogs, and small,
noisy boys. Sun-dappled creeks with shaded pools under the
root masses of great cottonwoods and soft maples, and maybe
grapevines to climb and leap from. When such creeks run out
into open fields, their inner bends are often shaggy with grasses
and coarse weeds where the tractors cannot reach—the only real
wildlife cover in some totally cultivated landscapes. This is
where the quail covey will be, and perhaps a deer, and muskrat
and coon trails through the grass between cornfield and creek,
haunted by mink and red fox. Exciting places to the naturalist,
but the river-wreckers are very businesslike about such things.
Their draglines feed on the farm creeks and streams, their
dredges wait to devour the Mississippi backwaters, and their
dams have stilled little limestone rivers.

Not far from my home in southwestern Illinois is a small
stream called Shoal Creek. In normal flow it probably averages

less than 40 feet wide, wandering down its wooded valley between deserts of corn and soybeans. A hard-bottomed, productive little stream, much of it is overhung with soft maples that
shade and cool the water, their twisted root wads anchoring the
banks. Deep bends alternate with shallow riffles. The adjacent
woodlands are some of the best deer range left in the county,
and there are long canopied sloughs that produce countless
wood ducks. Last year, fisheries biologists rotenoned a hundred-
yard stretch of Shoal Creek that ended in a log drift. The hole
under that drift, only 52 inches deep, produced a number of
flathead catfish weighing up to 12 pounds, and many channel
catfish, crappies and sunfish. The biologists estimated that this
one pocket of Shoal Creek held the equivalent of 700 pounds of
catchable fish per river acre—a fantastic standing fishery.

A good place, but not good enough for the Soil Conservation
Service and the Army Corps of Engineers. Several years ago the
SCS channelized the upper end of Shoal Creek for twenty miles.
The Corps wanted to channelize much of the rest, killing the
stream on the way to its union with the Kaskaskia, but they
were stopped—for the time being.

Thousands of such creeks and rivers have caught the eyes of
the SCS and the Corps, and are scheduled for treatment. It is
brutal treatment, ruthless and efficient, converting natural flow-
ages like Shoal Creek into straight, featureless, high-banked
drainage ditches.

I have heard colonels of the Army Engineers speak glibly of
the quality recreation provided by their works—of the advantages of damming natural streams and exchanging canoes for
speedboats, and smallmouth bass for water-skiing. The Chief of
the Soil Conservation Service recently observed that channel
improvement "has very little adverse impact" on recreation
within a watershed, and that stream channelization can actually
benefit fishing, hunting, boating and canoeing.

He didn't say how. And the kids up there along the headwaters of Shoal Creek would like to know.

The Running Country

LIEUTENANT COLONEL STEPHEN KEARNY'S ORDERS were clear: proceed northwest into the Iowa wilderness with a unit of cavalry and survey the Des Moines River for possible fort sites.

They left Keokuk in June 1835 with a couple of transport wagons and a small herd of beef cattle, riding along the crest of a sun-drenched prairie ridge between the Des Moines and Skunk rivers, bound upstream into unknown country.

It was a beautiful time, as only an early prairie summer can be beautiful. The ridges glowed with flowers, and when the wind parted the new grass ahead, Kearny saw wild strawberries "that made the whole track red for miles" and stained the horses' hooves and fetlocks.

Slowed by the wagons and cattle, the party was averaging fifteen miles each day. As it turned out, that was about the same rate that the strawberries were ripening; the soldiers and the berry ripening were traveling north together. As if that weren't lucky enough, one of the cows freshened and began giving milk, and the troop dined on fresh strawberries and cream all the way to the headwaters of the Des Moines.

First-class foraging, and it sure beat beans. But then, this strange new country beat almost anything.

It was virgin tallgrass prairie, and Kearny and his men rode stirrup-deep through young bluestem grass and flowers, the hooves muffled in a loamy wealth that had been accruing annual interest for twenty thousand years. Later that summer, when they skirted ridges and crossed flats, their horses would vanish in a sea of Indian grass and big bluestem so tall that it could be tied in knots across the pommel of a cavalry saddle. It was a land belonging to grass, flowers, and sun, a new sort of land that was open to the sky, and trees and shadows shrank from it. For a long time, so did people.

The first signs of prairie began back in Ohio as little natural clearings in the great eastern hardwood forest. They were strange clearings filled with strange grasses, and they saved a lot of axework. These eastern outriders of the prairie were quickly filled with fields and people, and vanished before men had a chance to really know them.

Scattered openings continued across northern Indiana, becoming larger, although the land was mostly forest. And then suddenly, twenty miles west of the Wabash River, the world opened up. A man would walk up out of the forested floodplain, step through a screen of sumac and wild plum, and stand blinking in a land that blazed with light and space. He was at the eastern edge of the Grand Prairie of Illinois; from there, north to Lake Michigan and west to the Mississippi, the prairies opened and broadened, sometimes spanning fifty miles without a tree or any other object to break the fabric of the grassland.

From the Wabash, this tallgrass prairie ran to the Missouri River and beyond, covering the western parts of Missouri and Minnesota and almost all of Iowa, extending into the eastern Dakotas, deep into Nebraska, and down into Kansas, Oklahoma, and Texas. It was called *tallgrass prairie* because it was a region dominated by huge grasses—Indian grass, the cordgrasses, and big bluestem, which might grow twelve feet high. It was a special region, labeled clearly and precisely with special plants. At its western boundary, out around the 100th meridian, the tallgrass prairie merged with shorter mixed grasses and mid-grasses, which merged in turn with the short grasses of the Great Plains.

True prairie was not a matter of location, but of composition. The lie of the land had nothing to do with whether it was prairie or not; if it was tallgrass prairie it included the tallgrass communities. Some prairie was flat, much of it was rolling, and some was broken and rocky. But it needed tallgrasses if it was to qualify as true prairie—the most easterly of the great American grassland societies that sprawled between the Rockies and the eastern forests.

It was here that the forested East ended, and the West really began. It stunned the pioneers coming from their Ohio and Kentucky forests, and one old journal effused: "The verdure and flowers are beautiful, and the absences of shade and the consequent profusion of light, produces a gaiety which animates every beholder."

Open as it was, it was not treeless. My home country in Iowa was a series of named prairies, such as the Ross Prairie or the Posegate Prairie, or whatever, and these stretches of shaggy grass were more or less fenced with groves and timbered valleys. Such prairies were said to resemble lakes, with boundary timber as shorelines indented with deep vistas like bays and inlets, throwing out long points that were capes and headlands.

Years ago, when Americans were less homogenized and outlandish accents still drew attention, a man in Maine asked me where I hailed from. I told him I was from Iowa. He shuddered, and calc'lated that his forests and hills must seem very beautiful to me. I replied that it was sure different from anything back in Story County, all right, and that seemed to please him.

The truth of it was, my home country had about all the hills and trees that we needed.

Our prairie country had a marked pitch and roll to it, like an ocean quieting after a bad storm. There is prairie country that's about as flat as land can be, but most prairie has a fine roll and break, with the land billowing off to the skyline and some timber down in the folds.

Many of the original trees were the same as back East: elms, hard maples, silver maples, shagbark hickories. But in Iowa, the beech tree's place was taken by basswood; I never saw a beech until I was thirty years old.

The prairie forests varied, depending on where you found them. Along smaller streams were wild plum, box-elder, wild cherry, soft maple, elm, and wild grape. If the floodplain was flat and wide, there were walnuts, hackberries, and great cottonwoods. These floodplain forests were densely undergrown, but this wasn't true of forest higher up on the ridges. There the trees were encroaching on prairie domain, and had to recognize the sovereignty of King Grass. These upland forests, what there were of them, were open. The groves of oaks and maples, huge-boled and ancient, looked like royal parks. The ground beneath them was free of undergrowth and carpeted with shade-tolerant grasses and flowers. Those old upland groves are gone today, mostly, but now and then you'll see a sentinel oak at the edge of a high pasture. After a hard rain, the closely grazed ground on such a ridge may glitter with flint flakes—the tribes knew good summer camps when they saw them.

Primeval prairie woods were found on sand or clay ridges, rocky outcrops, or the floodplains of streams. All the richest parts of the original prairie country were in grass; the forest existed at the sufferance of grass, and only on places that grass did not choose to occupy.

I've never thought of such country as monotonous, although my Maine friend would have felt so, I'm sure. But I've had four generations to get the forest out of my blood. By 1800, some of my people had begun to peer warily out of the Ohio forests; by 1825 they had gotten as far west as the eastern edge of the Grand Prairie. Bit by bit, they crept out of the trees and weaned themselves away from the Wooden Country. In 1853 my great-grandad grasped the nettle (and a new bride) and left the old states, heading west into the prairie frontier of central Iowa.

The strain has bred true; I like to return to trees, and sit and walk and hunt under them, but I could never live under them if they kept out all the sky.

Those royal groves must have been something, though.

Why all that grass?

Why, suddenly, twenty miles west of the Wabash, did the land begin running out of trees?

Some early settlers thought the land was just too poor to grow trees—but it didn't take them long to find that wasn't true. They finally decided that prairie was caused and maintained by the fall and spring infernos that swept through the grasslands, leaving leagues of blackened ash and carbonizing any tree seedling that had the temerity to invade prairie.

There was a lot to this. Certain islands in prairie lakes had fine groves of ash trees where fire could never reach. Yet the fire theory had gaps in it, and some early ecologists began to suspect that fire was an effect of prairie rather than a cause.

Mostly, it was a matter of rainfall. Eastern forests are in humid climate while grasslands are in drier country. The plains and prairies lie in the rain shadow of the Rocky Mountains—a lofty barricade to the moisture-laden winds from the Pacific. Prevailing winds carry enough rain to grow grass, but not unlimited forests. Then, too, prairie maintains itself well. Even at the eastern edge of the grassland, where rainfall was sufficient to support either tallgrasses or trees, the dividing line was abrupt. Tallgrass prairie is a closed community that rarely admits aliens; tree seedlings can seldom live in prairie sod with its intense competition, crowding, and ground-level shading.

Years ago, a pioneer ecologist named Bohumil Shimek began to suspect that the grasslands weren't just caused by low rainfall and maintained by fire, but resulted from evaporation caused by incessant exposure to wind, low relative humidity, and frequent high temperatures.

One of the greatest of these, Professor Shimek felt, was wind. Wind breaks twigs and leaves, and drives dust and sand against delicate tissues, abrading and tearing them. The effect of constant wind on tree leaves is also physiological. Shaking a plant increases its rate of transpiration—in a climate where a tree can't afford to transpire too much water vapor. Of course, this is checked by the closing of the leaves' stomata. But that also checks the processes of respiration and assimilation. If physical shaking continues long and violently, the plant can be weakened and even killed.

It follows, then, that trees most exposed in their spring and summer leaf seasons to hot, constant winds would be in the greatest danger.

This is apparent in Iowa, where spring and summer winds often blow from the southwest. Western Iowa streams that drain into the Missouri flow southwest, directly into these winds. Eastern Iowa streams flowing into the Mississippi run southeast—at right angles to the prevailing winds and with maximum protection. Iowa streams flowing southwest may have scanty, brushy timber if they have trees at all, and some flow for miles through open prairie. The Maple, Little Sioux, Boyer, and Nishnabotna are examples. In eastern Iowa, the southeast-flowing streams—the Cedar, Wapsipinicon, Des Moines, Iowa, and Skunk—have dense floodplain forests.

In western Illinois we can see the effects of wind and sun on the hills above the Mississippi. Certain forested headlands and bluffs above the river are capped with little tallgrass prairies. You won't find these on east-facing hillsides, looking away from the river. The hill prairies face west, at right angles to the full blaze of an August afternoon, looking out over a broad floodplain where the wind has a long fetch. Of all our Illinois landscapes, none are more exposed to intense sun and wind than these west-facing river bluffs and hills. They are ecological niches of native prairie.

The steep ground that creates these prairies may also protect them. Some of the limestone river bluffs near my home are nearly two hundred feet high, towering over the Great River Road and the Mississippi in white, buttressed walls. The edges of these cliffs are dangerous pastures, as some farmers have found. Cows, unlike cats, can't land on their feet nor spare eight lives. Just behind these river bluffs may be rough, wooded valleys that discourage any farming. Guarded from front and behind, the little prairies along the brinks of these river cliffs have survived.

Our family often goes up there for Sunday lunches, climbing gargantuan limestone stairs to the clifftop. With forest at our backs and the broad Mississippi out in front, we bask in original bluestem high above the beaten highway of a newer, noisier world.

The old-time prairie was a grandmother's quilt of color and form that shifted constantly as the wind breathed life into the grasses. Willa Cather remembered Nebraska when "there was so much motion to it; the whole country seemed, somehow, to be running." One of Harvey Dunn's finest paintings of prairie life was of a Dakota girl pumping water, her skirts blowing, an embodiment of the old prairie adage: "There's just nothin' prettier than a girl pumping water in the wind!"

The play of wind on tallgrasses, with the land running beneath a towering sky, is something we may not know again, for we will not see such vistas of grass again.

The tallest of the prairie grasses—big bluestem and cordgrass or slough grass—never reached their highest growth in the richest soil, but in lower, marshier land. There, where substrata of clay lay near the surface, the big bluestem grew to twelve feet. Cows could be lost in it, and might be found by a mounted man only when he stood in the saddle or rode up a nearby ridge and watched for the cows moving through the deep grass. The size of prairie grass was proportional to moisture. The dark green slough grass, called "rip-gut" because of its saw-edged leaves, grew in dense stands on low flats. Pioneers avoided low prairie swales that were marked by this "black grass." A traveler had to pick his way carefully over the ridges in spring, for the low places were impassable. When incumbent frontier politicians made soaring reelection promises, they often swore that they had "waded sloughs" in the interests of their constituents, for no work was harder than that.

Another lowland grass was Indian grass—tall, coarse, and up to eight feet high, usually found in more southerly regions of tallgrass prairie. All of these are fine livestock feeds, and make excellent hay if cut before their stems are too tough and fibrous.

The higher and better-drained the prairie became, the finer

and shorter the grasses. True prairie uplands are dominated by little bluestem, with rich stands of Junegrass, side-oats grama, needlegrass, and prairie dropseed.

The tallgrasses need moisture and plenty of it, and were the dominant grasses in the prairies east of the Mississippi. Farther west, as rainfall diminished, tallgrasses retreated to lower parts of the prairie, and the well-drained uplands were covered with shorter midgrasses. Still farther west, with even less rainfall, those midgrasses were replaced by the shortgrasses of the true plains: western wheatgrass, buffalo grass, and blue grama.

Colors and texture of tallgrass prairies varied with the season and elevation. In early spring, the bleak prairie hillsides might be brownish gray from the weathered ash of the fall fires. Then, often well before Easter, the prairie pasqueflowers would appear. Of all early wildflowers these are the bravest, not blooming in sheltered woods, but out in the big open on glacial moraines where the wind cuts to the bone in late March.

Then, one bright morning, the south-facing slopes would look as if patches of spring sky had fallen on them, and you knew that the bird's-foot violets were in bloom. There was white, woolly, prairie cat's-foot coming on, and the first green blush of new grass on the slopes.

The hilltops were splashed with early spring flowers: false dandelion, cream-colored paintbrush, and mats of groundplum vetch. The new grass would be spangled with tiny purple, blue, and white grass flowers, and perhaps yellow upland buttercups and yellow lousewort.

When the bluestem grasses began to appear in mid-April it was a signal for the spring flowers to hurry, for they were small plants that were easily overpowered by the growing grasses.

Prairie and meadow violets appeared, with vetch and false indigo. Along the streams and low places were marsh marigold, yellow stargrass, and purple heart-leaved violets. The prairie pinks came into bloom and enameled a landscape of young grass with pink, white, and purple. With them came the puccoons, splashes of rich orange in the greens and pinks.

By early June, most of the spring flowers were gone. The

flowers were taller now. Daisies began to appear, and larkspur and purple coneflower. There was a foot-high prairie lily with a red bloom, and with these lilies came clouds of prairie roses. About the only thing that "them politicians down at Des Moines" ever did that pleased our Grandma Tut was to make the prairie rose Iowa's state flower.

By summer there were myriads of blossoms, all holding their own with the lofty grasses. Wild indigo, with its heavy, creamy blooms, stood tall. White larkspur stood above many grasses; so did oxeye daisy, many sunflowers, goldenrod, and compass-plant—the set of its oaklike leaves marking the prairie meridian. Leadplant, with its silver-gray leaves and purplish flowers, was everywhere on the upland prairie. From August on through autumn, wild asters bloomed white, lavender, and purple. Deep in the ripening grasses, almost hidden, were the fringed gentians and bottle gentians.

This was the season when the prairie flamed with blazing-star or gayfeather, a tall purple spike of blooms whose root bulbs were fed to Indian ponies to increase speed and endurance.

Some of the finest floral displays were on low ground, hidden around the prairie marshes. Pioneers recall four types of wild orchids there. The smallest, and possibly the rarest, was yellow. There was a white orchid with purple mottling, and a larger yellow orchid. The largest and finest of the wild orchids in Iowa grew two feet high far back in the marshes; on each stalk there were two or more white and purple blooms with subdued mottling, and floral pouches "big enough to hide a hummingbird."

The prevailing colors of prairie flowers were white, purple, and yellow, although some phloxes came in tints of red, and there were red lilies and the orange-red butterfly weed with its masses of tiny hourglass-shaped flowers. The first of the year's prairie flowers were the smallest and most delicate; as the seasons went on, flowers became taller, gaudier, and stronger-stemmed to compete with the rising tide of grasses that deepened and coarsened with the summer.

In color and form, those grasses had the last word. By Indian summer they had ripened, rich and stately, each clan with its own colors, and those colors shifting and changing with the wind. By September the grasses had lost their greens and had deepened into tones of gold and bronze. There were tawny stands of ripe Indian grass, patches of airy switchgrass heavy with seed, and the wine-red fields of bluestem. The colors did not last; as winter came on the grasses bleached and faded as the prairie world retrenched, sending its vigor underground, to await spring and the time of pasqueflowers.

This tallgrass prairie swarmed with wildlife.

It wasn't uniform, featureless range. There was a variety of habitats: ridgetops with short midgrasses, hillsides and flats with deep grasses, upland groves, heavily timbered floodplains, and the endless sumac and plum woods borders.

Out on the open ground there were bison, although probably never as many as on the shortgrass plains farther west. There were bear, ruffed grouse and turkey in the forests, and deer and elk in and around the forest edges.

The prairie then was strewn with small lakes, potholes, and marshes, and veined with tiny creeks that ran over beds of bright glacial pebbles, hidden beneath the arching grasses. The openness of these prairies, and their frequent wetness, drew countless shorebirds and waterfowl. The prairies teemed with ducks, geese, pelicans, sandhill cranes, whooping cranes, bitterns, egrets, and whistling swans. Shorebirds came in vast spring clouds; in March and April, golden plovers began arriving from Argentina on their way to the Arctic, and they would always stop on the prairie. These plovers (settlers called them "prairie pigeons") hunted burned hillsides for grubs and insect eggs, and the dark slopes were spangled with moving gold and silver as the great flocks of plovers fed.

Swans and geese arrived in squadrons to graze on the new bluestem shoots, and with them came huge, loose wedges of Eskimo curlews, long-billed curlews, and upland plovers.

Even without trees, the prairie drew songbirds. The bobolink was one of the old-timers, and so was the kingbird. There was our western meadowlark, singer laureate of the tallgrass prairie, almost identical with the eastern meadowlark but singing a longer and more tuneful song. Lacking trees, the meadowlarks and dickcissels and song sparrows made do, and sang from tall flower stalks; many of the grasslanders, such as longspurs, horned larks, and bobolinks, simply sang on the wing.

Some prairie women sorrowed at leaving their eastern song-birds behind them in the forests, but this began to change as homestead windbreaks of soft maples, box-elders, and willows began to mature. The "timber birds" did some pioneering of their own, and joined the settlers out on the prairie. Many prairie-born children could easily remember the first robins that they ever saw—an event marked not only by a brand-new bird, but by the delight of their parents.

Such are the accounts that come to us, recalling the old prairie as a place rich in form, life, and color—a trans-Mississippi Eden that was fresh and new. (Many of these writers returned East to do their euphuizing.)

But there were those who hated prairie, and spoke of it as "a fearful place."

Washington Irving wrote: "To one unaccustomed to it, there is something inexpressibly lonely in the solitude of a prairie. The loneliness of a forest seems nothing to it. There the view is shut in by the trees and the imagination is left to picture some livelier scene beyond. But here we have the immense extent of landscape without a sign of human existence . . ."

The prairie had many faces, and men saw them in different ways. But whatever the prairie's variables, there were some constants. Big, it was, and overwhelming. Lonely, it was.

The second wave of pioneers, passing through tiny settlements on the prairie frontier, were greeted with pathetic eagerness by the original settlers, who implored them to stop and stay. Some of this was a practical need for neighbors; much was loneliness. But the greater part may have been a profound insecurity—of being part of something wholly new, with no ancestral precedents in Europe or New England. In a forest a man is partly hidden; he has carved a niche with sheltering hills and walls of trees. There is intimacy in a forest. But not on a

prairie; there are no walls on a prairie. The prairie man and
woman, and their puny fields, were exposed to a vast and
pitiless sky. There was no snugness, no security, nothing to
shield the family; a man was alone and naked, bared to an
openness of terrifying intensity and magnitude.

It must have been hardest for women, for they have the
deepest and most tender roots in tradition. The prairie men left
many things in the East and good riddance to most of them, the
stump farms and taxes and fields that were more rock than soil.
But a woman left the church were she had been married; she left
a stone-and-frame home with a rock maple by the kitchen
window, and familiar birdsong, and followed her man into a
heathen wilderness of cyclones, blizzards, flaming horizons, and
an everlasting wind that would turn her skin to leather and end
her youth.

Even as the people changed the prairie, it changed them. That
prairie and the vastness beyond it were uniquely American. The
men and women who settled there were also unique, or became
so, and they may have been the first total, genuine Americans.
They were new people in a new land—and such people and land
had not been known before.

It was, as the people finally found, a land of incredible richness
and fecundity.

At first, they deduced that if the land was too poor to grow
trees it was probably too poor to grow much in the way of
crops—overlooking the point that their crops were actually
grasses, and that the prairie was the world's finest grower
of grasses.

That was one reason the first of the prairie pioneers settled in
bottomland timber. It was the logical thing to do. Forests had
building materials and fuel, clear streams and abundant game.
Then, too, these settlers were accustomed to clearing fields from
forest—that was simply the way men farmed. They failed to see
that trees grew on the prairie's poorest soils, and that forest soils
were a thin veneer of fertility that was a delusion, for it would
be quickly eroded away when there were no longer trees to

stabilize it. Finally, the early settler didn't know how to cope with open prairie, and he was terrified of the prairie fires that did not enter the bottomland forests.

So, for a long time, home base remained in the timber, and familiar forest was laboriously cleared in preference to breaking virgin prairie sod. In Marshall County, Iowa, as late as 1867, prairie was selling for $3 to $10 per acre while timbered lands sold for $30 to $50. This was the first stage in prairie pioneering, with families living in forested clearings as they had always done, farming some small fields, grazing some livestock, and hunting and trapping.

But in spite of the prairie's strangeness, the pioneer farmers soon found that it was where the action was. They left the trees and began to learn what the land really offered.

Building was one of the first and greatest problems. Forests were often miles distant, and there were no railroads to bring building materials, so the settlers had to invent. In the western parts of the longgrass prairie they built with sod, cutting thick turfs a foot wide and two feet long. A course would be laid two sods wide; the next course would be at right angles to the first. This sealed all joints, and the wall of a sod house would be from two to three feet thick, warm in winter and cool in summer. The roofs, made of pole framing, would be covered with thin turfs and perhaps thatched with slough grass. This same cordgrass served as fuel; tightly twisted into faggots, it would burn hotly as long as ten minutes. In one hour a prairie boy or girl could twist a day's supply of fuel. Years later, their grandchildren would gather corncobs from the hog lot for the kitchen range. In one form or another, grass cooked and heated.

Some "soddies" were grand, two-storied, shingle-roofed houses, and a sod home with touches of Victorian architecture was about as wild a concession to function and fashion as we'll ever know. But as lumber became available at reasonable prices in the 1870s and 1880s, and freighters and railroads began bringing in lumber and glass, sod houses began to vanish.

The second great problem was sodbreaking. The native sod was a solid mass of locked, intertwined rootlets that were studded with the massive rootstocks of compassplant, redroot, and other forbs.

There were commercial plowmen who would break your claim for $12.25 per acre with a "breaking plow"—a huge, wheeled device drawn by five-yoke of oxen that cut a furrow two feet wide. The moldboard of the old bar share-breaking plow was seven feet long.

A breaking plow could also be made from the wheels of the settler's wagon, a handmade axle, and a long beam that could be raised or lowered to regulate the depth of the furrow. Still, there was the problem of the moldboard. Eastern plows had great, heavy, cast-iron moldboards that were designed for the rocky fields of New England. They were almost useless on the prairie, for they would not "scour" and rid themselves of clinging loam.

A great breakthrough came in 1837 when John Deere of Illinois invented his new prairie plow. It was a walking-plow that could be drawn through prairie sod with a three-horse team—a handsome implement, light and artistic, with a bright, shining, tempered steel moldboard. It was one of those great pieces of original art that combine utility with beauty, like the Lancaster rifle or the gracefully curved helve of our American ax.

With such a plow, the farmer could break the dense prairie sod with amazing efficiency. As the furrow was cut, there was a constant popping sound, like a tiny volley of pistol shots, caused by the breaking of tough roots and spurs. This incessant cracking and popping had a slight ring to it, amplified by the tempered steel of the polished moldboard.

It was best to break new ground between early May and mid-July. The sod was plowed as shallow as possible; the thinner it was cut, the better it would rot. A settler might strike an ax into the sod and drop seed into the hole, and while the overturned sod was decomposing and mellowing it was also nourishing the growing corn. Or, you could drop corn into every fourth row while plowing, and this would be covered by the plowing of the fifth row. Neither the yield nor the quality of corn was high that first year, but it was sufficient, and a man might make fifteen to twenty-five bushels per acre of "sod corn."

It might be several years before the grassroots had completely rotted and become rich, smooth loam. But it was all worth it. A man could spend half his lifetime back in the Wooden Country clearing land and just getting ready to farm. On the prairie, one man and his team, working for only two months, could have an "eighty" broken and planted with sod corn or flax.

It was a hard and lonely life for the prairie families that came first, but there were neighbors on the way. During one month in 1854, over 1,700 covered wagons passed near Peoria, Illinois, bound for Iowa. The real pioneering era of Iowa's frontier—the sod shanty and semisubsistence living—lasted no more than a decade.

But during the years of primitive abundance, there were strange and primitive dangers.

Unlike trees and shrubs, the tops of annual grasses die each autumn. Chlorophyll fades, and life retreats into the roots, rhizomes, and seeds of the grass. The dead materials left above may return to the earth. Or, in a sense, to the sun.

Tall prairie grasses, especially in dry autumns, became tinder of almost explosive quality. Prairies have always burned from fires set by lightning, and sometimes by man. Indians were known to fire the prairies to drive game or defend themselves from enemies. Settlers commonly caused fires that they blamed on the Indians. But whatever the cause, one thing was sure: each autumn and spring the fires would come.

By day there might be a strange haze in the air, and a smokiness flowing down the watersheds. By night, a reddish-orange glow was reflected from behind the horizons. If there was no wind, the haze and the glow might last for days before the settler actually saw flames, and he had time to plow firelanes around his buildings and stack-yards, and burn the grass within the plowing. The windless prairie fire would advance deliberately, marching across the grassland while tufts of bluestem vanished in puffs of flame, the white smoke drifting into blue sky. Coyotes and foxes exploited this, hunting before the flames to catch dispossessed mice and rabbits.

But if there was wind, there was a fire blizzard—one of the greatest horrors of prairie life.

It came with walls of flame thirty feet high and a deep devouring roar, and black smoke instead of white, and the sun darkened and animals went mad. The glow of these great prairie fires could be seen for forty miles, and showers of ash and flake would be carried that far ahead by the wind. Single prairie fires were known to have burned over two hundred square miles, and one fire traveled over twenty-two miles "as fast as a horse could run."

Within five miles of where I was born, a family of five Ohio emigrants died on a lovely October day in 1860 when they were trapped in a ravine by prairie fire.

In 1873, in Saline County, Nebraska, a fire blizzard roared across the grasslands toward a prairie schoolhouse. A mother who lived in a nearby soddy ran over to the school for her own children and some young relatives. The teacher begged her not to take them, but the hysterical mother would not listen. The ten children and the woman tried to outrun the fire, but lost their race. All eleven died in the flames. The teacher and the other pupils were safe on a nearby plowed field, and the school never did burn.

Old Sitting Bull himself, in the dry, flaming autumn of 1885, warned some Dakota schoolchildren that they could never run away from a prairie fire. "Go to bare ground," he counseled them, "or onto sand, gravel, or plowing. Or set a backfire. Go to a place with no grass. But do not run."

Entire towns were destroyed by some of these prairie fires; in Leola, South Dakota, all but twelve of the town's hundred buildings were burned in 1889 by a prairie fire that traveled forty miles in four hours.

Prairie fires were feared by almost every pioneer, and even the small boys who usually found them exciting had to admit there were drawbacks. Herbert Quick, the Iowa writer, told of the sharp grass stubs on burned-over prairie that pricked a school-boy's bare feet and caused festering sores. Of course, this could have been solved by simply wearing shoes to school, but that's a stupid solution when it's spring and you're ten years old and the prairies are greening up. Those prairie boys found a friend in need in the pocket gopher. The big gophers threw up mounds of soft, fine, cool earth, often in long lines. The ultimate luxury was to walk all the way to a country school without stepping off a soft gopher mound. It never worked that way, of course. The gopher mounds usually wandered off in the wrong direction and a boy ended up walking farther to school through grass stubs than if he'd taken a direct route in the first place.

That problem, like all others caused by prairie fires, vanished with the bluestem. There came a time when the autumn horizons no longer glowed red at night, for the prairie was gone.

We spent our tallgrass prairie with a prodigal hand, and it probably had to be that way, for these are the richest farm soils in the world. There were certain wilderness things that were fated to be spent almost to the vanishing point: bison in short-grass plains, lobos and grizzlies in settled cattle country—and the vistas of true prairie.

But spending is one thing; bankruptcy is another.

To squander the last stands of true prairie would wipe out a valuable index to original quality. It is important that our agronomists, botanists, zoologists, and soil physicists have reference points to the original plants and soils of our most valuable ecosystem. We may someday have to rebuild those soils, or try to. Native prairie is a baseline from which creative research can depart, and return for reference. We'd never dream of melting down the platinum meter in Paris and converting it to jewelry; it is the master rule, an original measurement upon which so much engineering and science are based. And so, in an even greater sense, is native prairie.

Just as important is the maintenance of certain tangible links with the old time. To destroy the last of the native prairie would be as criminally stupid as burning history books, for prairie is a chronicle of human courage, endurance, and victory, as well as a finished natural system.

Deciding sometime tomorrow afternoon that maybe we should have a few more prairies around, and then abandoning a few cornfields to that end, just won't get it. Original tallgrass prairie is the endpoint of twenty-five million years of evolution; it cannot be restored overnight, if indeed it can be restored at all. If the job of prairie restoration were left to nature alone, and if there were adequate sources of seed, nature might be able to convert cornfields to "native" prairie in two hundred to three hundred years. Imitation prairies have been built, but with perhaps thirty plant species instead of the original two hundred or more, each occupying a special niche in a special way. Prairie in its full form cannot be reconstructed by man—Eric Hoffer notwithstanding.

However, tallgrass prairie is the most difficult of all native America to conserve. This is because it is the world's most valuable farm soil—and it must be conserved in quantity if it is to mean what it should. There are still many "splinter prairies" in Midwestern states, some of several hundred acres. A man could stand in a grove of virgin white pine of the same size and feel that he was in primeval forest. Not so with prairie. To the average man, a scrap of native prairie is just a shaggy weedpatch between cornfields. Prairie must have sweep and perspective to look like prairie. It is more than just native grasses and forbs; it is native sky, and native horizons that stretch the eye and the mind. To be prairie, really good prairie, it must embrace the horizons. That is the ideal, and the only places where you will still find it are in parts of Nebraska's Sand Hills and in the Flint Hills of eastern Kansas.

The Flint Hills prairie has survived because beds of cherty limestone lie so close to the surface that the land can't be plowed. It is heavily grazed, and has been for a hundred years, but it is still prairie, rolling in long waves from the Nebraska line down into the Osage Hills of Oklahoma. It's country worth seeing.

One morning early last April, Kansas biologists Bob

McWhorter and Bob Henderson hauled me out of bed at 3:00
A.M. for a prairie chicken count in the northern Flint Hills.

Before dawn we were on the ancient dancing grounds of the
prairie chicken, with a traditional stage setting. The southern
horizon was flame-torn with spring prairie fires that reddened
the sky and gave the strange impression of sunset at dawn.
Somewhere behind us several coyotes were swapping hunting
yarns and settling down for the day, and even before it was light
enough to see, we could hear the haunting, hollow booming of
prairie chickens from several directions, some nearby and others
dim with distance. With first light we could see them on the
prairie ridge before us, over thirty of them in the closest flock,
the sun glowing orangely on the inflated air sacs of the dancing,
posturing males. As we watched, a phalanx of upland plovers
swept past. Just over the ridgetop to the north, not twenty yards
above the fire-blackened prairie that was beginning to blush
green with new bluestem, a column of Canada geese moved out
for breakfast. Another prairie day had begun, much the same as
spring days have begun on Kansas prairies since the Miocene.

Of the relic prairies that I know, none is as poignant as the tiny
scrap that I found years ago in the center of an intensely farmed
Iowa section.

It was a small, lost graveyard, all that remains of the little
settlement of Bloomington, wiped out by diphtheria over a
hundred years ago. About a dozen weathered stone markers
leaned and lay in a patch of original bluestem. Among the graves
were those of a young mother and her children, and when I
found the place in late summer their graves were set about with
a few tall, magenta torches of blazing-star, stateliest of all prairie
flowers. It was part of an original time and place, and it held
fitting memorials. There were the flowers of gayfeather to lift
the spirits of lonely, beauty-starved women. There was bluestem for the men, for their haycutting and prairie chicken hunting; for the children, there was compassplant, with its wonderful
chewing gum, and wild strawberrries hidden in the grass.

That patch of tallgrass prairie was a more enduring memorial

than the stones that stood there, and infinitely more appropriate. Today, our memorials reflect our values, and we will probably be interred in manicured "memory gardens," our graves
decked with plastic blossoms that are imitations of imitations.
That, too, may be appropriate.

My feeling for tallgrass prairie is like that of a modern man who
has fallen in love with the face in a faded tintype. Only the
frame is still real; the rest is illusion and dream. So it is with the
original prairie. The beautiful face of it had faded before I was
born, before I had a chance to touch and feel it, and all that I
have known of the prairie is the setting and the mood—a broad
sky of pure and intense light, with a sort of loftiness to the days,
and the young prairie-born winds running past me from open
horizons.

   A strong place puts a mark on all that lives there, and the
mark may outlast the place itself. Prairie people are like their
western meadowlarks, seeming to be the same as their eastern
relatives, but with a different song. It was the prairie that
changed all that. It gave them a new song, and a new reason for
singing.

The Prairie Blizzard

IN THE MID–1850S, WITH ALL THAT EMPTY PRAIRIE west of the Mississippi and all those full purses east of the Ohio, land promoters soared to heights of commercial eloquence that haven't been attained since.

The emigrants' gazetteers and homesteaders' manuals glowed with superlatives. It was said that prairie men were devout and industrious, their women comely and virtuous, the children sturdy and obedient, and even their bulldogs were handsomer than the average run. The prairies were rich beyond mortal belief, with moderate and salubrious climate. It was a region, as one handbook breathlessly revealed, "with more birds' nests than rocks."

William Cullen Bryant, who had never seen a Western prairie in his life, effused:

These are the gardens of the desert, these
  The unshorn fields, boundless and beautiful,
For which the speech of England has no name—
  The Prairies.

Which is hard to top; when William Cullen Bryant effused on
something, it had been properly effused on .

But out in Iowa, an old-timer named William Haddock—who
had first come to the prairies in 1855—offered his own version
for winter reading:

These are the terror of the settlers, these,
   The Arctic blasts, howling and freezing,
For which the land of England has no name—
   The Blizzards.

Haddock knew what Bryant did not know, and what the
promoters didn't care to admit: that the prairies, so rich and
open and promising, levied certain cruel taxes. There was the
ceaseless wind, and emptiness. There were tornadoes, wildfires,
and diphtheria. But cruelest of all was winter. Not every winter,
maybe, but that one winter in five or six—that blizzard winter,
when the horizons vanished and a blinding white wall swept
down out of the northwest to scourge the grasslands. They were
killer storms, these winter cyclones for which England has no
name.

Today they are easily forecast, and warnings are televised into
every home by weathergirls who have wrought one of the
wonders of our age, and actually lent sex appeal to weather
reports. But until yesterday, the prairie blizzard was a fearful
blow that fell with almost no warning. We grew up in Iowa with
tales of farm children who perished on their way home from
country schoolhouses. Grandma Tut told us of farmers who tied
ropes between house and barn to guide them on the long,
dangerous journey that might be only fifty yards. There were
settlers who did not do this—and whose frozen bodies were
found weeks later far out on the prairie.

For many years, the standard by which all other prairie winters were scaled was the winter of 1856-57. This was the Massa-
cre Winter that wiped out the last of northern Iowa's big game—
and at least one frontier settlement.

Beginning in early fall, 1856, recurrent blizzards were followed
by slight thaws and deep cold. Deer and elk yarded in stream
valleys and were trapped by crusted drifts that would support

the weight of wolves and men, but not hooved animals. What starvation did not kill, the settlers did—with gun, ax, and even clubs and knives. It was many decades before deer returned to northwestern Iowa, and elk were gone forever.

That February, fifteen starving Sioux renegades drifted over into their old northwestern Iowa hunting grounds from South Dakota. They were the hardcore of frontier violence, led by the notorious Inkpadutah and including such outlaws as Old Man, Mysterious Father, Putting-On-Walking, and a Sisseton thug with the impressive name of Man-Who-Makes-A-Crooked-Wind-When-He-Runs. Instead of elk and deer, these Sioux found new settlers who had not only occupied the old hunting grounds but had even moved into the sacred Spirit Lake country. The enraged Indians massacred thirty-eight people—the entire settlement at Lake Okoboji

When the news reached Fort Dodge at the headwaters of the Des Moines River, a relief column was dispatched to Lake Okoboji. Most of the dead were found and buried. On the return march, the poorly equipped column was struck by an April blizzard. Two of the militiamen froze to death, several went snow-blind, and two went insane. The storms left drifts that lingered in some sheltered ravines until early June. Of such stuff were great-grandad's winters made.

Prairie winters are still made of the same stuff—sans the Indians and the deadly isolation. And when you pare it down to the basics, and face a prairie blizzard on even terms, you develop a great-grandad way of thinking. A lot of us did just that on Armistice Day, November 11, 1940.

It had begun as an unseasonably warm day in northern Iowa. But by midmorning the temperature was plummeting and a massive weather change was in the making, and John Cole and I figured it for a good day to jump-shoot mallards on the Skunk River.

We were tough and young, accustomed to about any kind of weather that our Iowa prairies offered. But we learned new things about weather that day. The temperature was dropping several degrees each hour, the sky darkening at midday, and the wind was building to a crescendo of bitter force. A hard, granu-

lar snow was driven horizontally, cutting and blinding any face
that was turned into it for long. Not even our hunting fever
could temper that terrible wind. We hunted north into the wind,
and the day resolved itself into small compartments of suffering.
The world about us was closed out by an encircling wall of wind
and snow; there were only Cole and I, and the fifty yards of
visible river that traveled with us, and the sheltered river bends
and the masses of ducks that cowered there.

The storm had caught a vast waterfowl migration over the
Midwest and had bludgeoned countless ducks down onto the
sloughs, ponds, and rivers. We saw mallards beyond number
that short day. Each sheltering riverbank had its huddled flock,
and some numbered into the hundreds. We would blunder up
on them and they would try to fly up into that roaring white-
ness, only to be battered back down onto the river. We would
fire at the rise, our eyes blinded with freezing tears, and the
sounds of our heavy 12-gauge guns were dim, muffled thuds
swept away on the wind.

Neither of us had hip boots. I remember that I wore heavy
blanket wool breeches with thick wool socks and short shoepacs, and we waded for the birds up to our hips. As we came out
of the water into that wind we would be quickly sheathed in ice
that sloughed off in plates as we walked. Evening came in late
afternoon and we were far upriver when we finally turned south
again, each with more than thirty pounds of mallards slung over
his shoulder, and that terrible wind pushing us homeward.

When we finally got there, exhausted and ravenous, we
walked into a parental storm about as violent as the one outside,
but much hotter. The folks had been listening to WHO (The
Voice of the Middlewest) on the old Majestic radio, and they
were pretty well worked up. The news was so bad that even
"Amos n' Andy" was interrupted by special bulletins. Hunters
were dying by dozens on the Upper Mississippi and northern
lakes and marshes, where waves were breaking over their blinds
and freezing or drowning them. We heard later that over forty
Midwestern hunters were killed by the storm.

Many blizzards have howled across the prairies since that

Armistice Day, but none have taken such a toll of human life. In fact, each succeeding winter finds the prairie people better equipped to deal with blizzards. Not so with wildlife, for the same technology that has made the prairie winters safe for men has redoubled their deadliness to wild creatures.

Prairie blizzards have always hit wildlife hard. Even the bison, facing into the gales with winterproofed heads and shoulders, suffered and died. Winter storms were probably one of the major checks that limited the vast herds before the arrival of gunpowder.

The blizzards can be tough on prairie deer, which may starve, freeze, or even smother if they can't find shelter. In the wake of one Dakota blizzard, a game biologist friend found a blinded fawn standing near a road, its face covered with a mask of ice. He caught the little deer easily, broke away its icy blindfold, and freed it. Prairie deer usually drift before a blizzard and seek shelter in river breaks or in timbered creek bottoms. If those timbered bottoms are narrow, as they usually are, they can become deathtraps where the deer perish in twenty-foot drifts that bury browse and shelter.

The tough little pronghorn antelopes seem better fitted to brave prairie blizzards than are deer, for pronghorns tend to avoid such deadly little valleys. Given any freedom of movement, antelope may move uphill toward higher ground where ridges are swept clear of snow. There they can usually survive in spite of cold and wind, for they are superbly equipped with thick coats of hollow hair. Herds of healthy antelope can be found feeding on open ridges after a blizzard has decimated local deer.

But it's another story if antelope are impeded by sheep-proof fences.

A barbed wire fence won't give an antelope much trouble, for the little speedster's solution to such an obstacle is to simply slide under the bottom strand—often at top speed, leaving a small cloud of hair floating off in the wind. This is not possible with a woven-wire fence meant to contain sheep. Unlike deer, most antelope will not jump over such fences. And so they drift helplessly along the fencelines and are often trapped in the cul-de-sac of a fencecorner by deepening drifts. The antelope may starve there, or freeze, or may simply be buried alive and suffocated, to be revealed after the next thaw as a standing, lifeless monument to a range made safe for sheep.

South Dakota's 1949 blizzard was a stark example of this fenced-antelope problem. Just north of Belle Fourche, in Butte County, lie the Owl Creek and Indian Creek ranges. It's good antelope country. It's also good sheep range, and is laced with sheep-proof fences that are part of the new look in sheep ranching. This is a direct result of predator control; with coyotes nearly wiped out of western South Dakota, there is no longer any great need for sheepherders, and sheep can be held more easily and cheaply behind woven wire.

That was the situation when the '49 blizzard hit the Owl Creek range. Something like 60 percent of the antelope perished behind the sheep-proof fences. In Harding County, the next county north, where the economy hinged more on beef than on wool, antelope losses were only a fraction as great. That was barbed-wire country, with three-strand fences that the antelope could sift through. And sift through they did, to safer blizzard range.

That 1949 blizzard, by the way, wiped out virtually every South Dakota pheasant west of the Missouri River.

It was nothing new; heavy blizzard kills of pheasants go back as far as the birds do. During the drought-scourged, shelterless winter of 1935-36, half of South Dakota's pheasants perished. It was even worse the following winter when over seventy inches of snow fell in northeastern South Dakota. Food and cover were buried deep under drifts, and 80 percent of the pheasants died. During the four winters from 1947 to 1950, nearly 1½ million pheasants died in South Dakota's snows.

The ring-necked pheasant is a very tough bird, in body and spirit. It adapts better to man and his doings than do any of the native prairie grouse, and is more tolerant of cultivation and heavy land use—up to a point. But the pheasant cannot make use of deep, soft snow as do native grouse that burrow into drifts where the temperature may be forty degrees warmer than the outer air. The pheasant takes potluck and simply roosts or huddles in what grassy cover it can find, and such prairie cover is a snowtrap, a drift-builder. Often, in the wake of a blizzard, food is not the pheasant's greatest problem. The scouring winds may blow fields free of snow and expose waste grain—but those same winds may bury roosting cover beneath towering drifts. And when the blizzard brings heavy snow that blankets the feeder fields as well, the hardy ringneck is forced into desperate action.

Such evicted pheasants may move into feedlots with cattle, or into barnyards with chickens. Or they may just strike out cross-country, moving as far as ten miles to better cover. This is a fantastic journey for a ring-necked pheasant that may normally live out its sedentary life on one section of land, and reflects the desperation of these birds. In a few cases, the moving pheasants do find cover. In most cases they do not, and they die, as 90 percent of the pheasants in southern Minnesota died in the winter of 1968-69.

The pheasants may freeze as snow is driven under wind-ruffled feathers, melted by the bird's body heat, and refrozen by the wind to sheathe the bird in ice. Some pheasants suffocate as snow is driven into their beaks and nostrils, slowly forcing their beaks open with growing balls of ice until the skin splits at the corners of their mouths. This seems to happen rarely with such natives as the sage grouse, sharptail, and prairie chicken. For one thing, they may be dug into a sheltering drift where the wind cannot reach them. In addition, some wildlifers observe that native grouse have feathered nostrils and may be immune to snow suffocation that can kill pheasants—whose nostrils are not feathered. Just speculation, but interesting.

Ducks and geese, when ambushed by a prairie blizzard, usually roll with the punch. By the time even an early blizzard strikes, adults and youngsters are well-dressed for the occasion, and a mallard or goose in winter plumage can withstand terrible weather.

Then, too, a blizzard rarely grounds waterfowl so long that they become famished and weak; long before that they are usually able to move out. And when a mallard or goose decides to move, he can make long and rapid transit. Mallards have been known to fly the 2,000 miles from southern Canada to Louisiana almost nonstop, making the trip in thirty-five hours.

They may not choose to go south at all, in spite of the weather. If there's a patch of open water somewhere and some picked cornfields blown clear of snow, a few mallards and geese may brave a prairie winter in spite of cold.

Many winters ago I was doing research on bottom fauna in the ooze of Little Wall Lake—a prairie lake in north-central Iowa. The temperature fell to B20° F. and there were times when I spudded through twenty inches of ice to take my bottom samples and oxygen determinations. Yet, there was a patch of open water on the far side of the lake that held a small flock of mallards. At the time, I assumed that the ducks had found a place where deep springs welled up and kept thick ice from forming.

The only other man on the lake was the late Paul Errington, who was working on muskrats. As far as Paul knew, there were no deep springs in that part of the lake. One bitter January day we slid his battered canoe over the edge of the ice and took depth temperatures in the open water. We could find no differences in water temperatures there or at any of my sample stations beneath the ice. It was apparent that the mallards themselves were keeping the area open, and they continued to do so until early February when a heavy snowfall covered the nearby cornfields. Then, in spite of moderating temperatures, the mallards pulled out—and the open water promptly froze.

Waterfowl have an option to stay north or head south, and it's a tribute to their adaptability and ruggedness that they stay north so often and for so long. The nonmigrant, nonhibernating species are not so fortunate. They have little latitude of action, and must bear the full brunt of the prairie winter with original equipment that is becoming increasingly inadequate.

Blizzards are a disagreeable inconvenience to man and may do him economic injury, but they rarely cause him mortal fear. They may still bury his stalled cars and even his freight trains beneath great drifts, but blizzard deaths today are more likely caused by heart attacks or carbon monoxide than by exposure. Each year, prairie winters grow more bearable for man and more unbearable for prairie wildlife. Each year, improved machines replace the farm boys who move to town, and with the progress of man's economy the iron land of the northern Midwest grows sterner and more barren and more unforgiving to the wildlife that struggles to survive the winters there.

Now and then, some federal program breathes new life into the winter prairies—but politicians pass and their programs pass with them. Through the 1950s and early 1960s the conservation reserve of the Soil Bank brought the old prairie look back to the cash grainbelt of the northern Midwest, and wildlife prospered in the lush new grasslands. But as Soil Bank contracts expired, so did these political prairies and much of the wildlife that they supported.

Also vanishing are the natural sloughs and prairie potholes with their havens of dense sedge. So are the shelterbelts near farmhouses. These little groves, found on the north side of every prairie farmstead, are not being replaced as they mature and die. Once they helped break the wind that beat furiously against the gaunt frame houses that were uninsulated except for the manure piled around their foundations. (Wonderful insulation that did double duty—warming the house as it fermented, and clearing the sinuses with zephyrs of ammonia.) Today, prairie houses are cleverly insulated and their central heating systems are fueled by big tanks of propane instead of cobs. Gone is the undergrown shelterbelt on the north side of the house where pheasants roosted on January nights in sixty degrees of frost—gone with the tented clumps of bluestem in the swales, and the dark slough grass of the potholes.

Almost every wild feature of the prairie has been tamed but one: the prairie winter. It is one of the few parts of the original that really persists. Its ferocity has been intensified by man, not abated—and the day could come when the blizzard is the only wild thing that moves across our winter prairies.

Where the River
Fits the Song

THERE'S A CERTAIN TIME, EARLY IN SPRING, when I begin feeling the pull of the river. It always comes when the willow slaps are greening up near Portage des Sioux, and the geese have gone on without me. The mighty Missouri, which joins the Mississippi not far from our back door, is running heavy and cold with distant snowmelt—and I know that the old river roads are open again.

The first pang comes on about March 20th, the anniversary of an 1822 ad that ran in the old St. Louis *Missouri Republican*:

"To enterprising young men. The subscriber wishes to engage one hundred young men to ascend the Missouri to its source, there to be employed for one, two, or three years. Wm. H. Ashley."

(I ain't no younker, Major Ashley, sir, and don't savvy "enterprising," but I'm a curly old wolf with a few howls left, and my stick floats upriver. Waugh!)

Another pang comes a little later, sometime around May 14th, if I happen to wander down to where Wood River once entered the Mississippi. There is a neglected little park there, still green and wooded but quieter than it was on that day in 1804 when William Clark and the Corps of Discovery left to cross the Mississippi and enter the mouth of the Missouri. I can sit within hailing distance of where, on that rainy spring morning, they broke camp and launched the two pirogues and the boat, bound for St. Charles to meet Captain Meriwether Lewis and then to vanish up the unknown river for over two years. Mid-May is a propitious time for such leave-taking, and it never comes but what I think of breaking my own winter camp and following.

This wouldn't be a hard place to leave. Behind me are the oil refineries of Wood River and Roxana, fouling the air in a desperate attempt to fuel the commerce of St. Louis—which is busily converting some of that energy to a pall of smog. And the best escape route lies directly across from me, where the broad Missouri emerges from under the point of St. Charles County. From the beginning it has been a prime escape route, the back door of a new republic that had doubled its size with the stroke of a quill pen. The Gateway Arch of St. Louis proclaims this to tourists, but the mouth of that muddy river over there is the real symbol of what it's all about.

As American rivers go, it has never looked like much. Not from this end, at least. Other rivers are more beautiful and imposing. But none can really compare with it—not the Potomac, nor Hudson, nor Columbia, nor even the Mississippi. The Missouri was a buckskin river, a wild Injun river drawing its medicine from the Big Sky. More men went up it than came back down—but they sent back the gold and beaver plew to prove that they got there. It was our true Northwest Passage at last, our only real westering river, the way into new empire. A great, brown, bank-caving, snag-toothed, turbulent bull buffalo of a river that muscled its way for 2,500 miles to close a river system between the Rockies and the snug farms of western Pennsylvania. The barriers of New France had crumbled, and the Missouri made its brag.

"Come on up! Why, I got places that you plowboys never dreamed of, where Hell fumes up out of the ground and Heaven sets on the mountaintop, where meat don't never spoil and the streams are stiff with beaver and the meadows black with elk. I come from where nothing's been used up and she's all new and shiny, and she's all free. If you're men enough to come, I'm river enough to bring you!"

And the men came, adding strokes of vermilion and ochre to the American Dream: Lewis and Clark and the Corps of Discovery, young Jim Bridger and old Hugh Glass, John Colter, Jed Smith, Bill Sublette, Jim Beckwourth, and a host of others whose names died with them.

The old colors haven't faded much; they are still bright and vivid.

Several years ago we attended a concert whose program included a choral arrangement of "Across the Wide Missouri." We were with some Eastern friends who, as far as we knew, had never seen the Missouri River. As the music ended there was a brief hush, and then the hall swelled with ovation. Our friends were applauding wildly, their eyes wet, which seemed a curious thing to one who has so often cussed the Big Muddy and had the river cuss back. Later, at supper, one of the ladies said: "Oh, that magnificent song! It should be our national anthem!" It wasn't just the song that she felt, of course, but what it celebrated—freedom still unused, all new and shiny.

As I sit downstream from where the mouth of Wood River used to be, sourly regarding the St. Louis waterfront, such romancing seems a bit foolish. The Missouri is a different river now, as most rivers are. The clouds of wild parakeets are gone from the floodplain forests—and many of those forests have been replaced by soybeans. The elk prairies are gone, too, replaced by corn, feedlots, and pastures. Today the lower river runs with the sewage of a hundred towns and cities, and the flushings of some of the greatest stockyards and packing plants in the world. There are wing dams, levees, and riprapped banks, and when the towns and cities grow more infrequent, the dams begin: Gavins Point, Fort Randall, Big Bend, Oahe, Garrison, and Fort Peck. Clearwater reservoirs that have drowned history are linked by docile stretches of river wandering past wheat-fields and farmtown junkyards. The original, free-flowing river has vanished from Missouri, Iowa, Nebraska, the Dakotas, and eastern Montana—and no amount of concert hall eulogy will bring it back.

Then what's to be done in mid-May, the time of leave-taking, when a gray-haired boy longs to follow an old escape route that he knows to be as tame and captive as he is? Dammit, I think, there's only one thing to do! Go far up, beyond the big dams and their synthetic lakes, up to where Lewis and Clark ended their second May on the river. Up to a place more distant from St. Louis now, in terms of time and change, than it was from St. Louis then. A fragment of original that John Colter would know, where the only engineers are beavers, and the river still fits its song.

There is such a place. Major Ashley, sir, here comes your curly wolf!

We have been on the river for six days. Our put-in was just below the mouth of the Marias River in north-central Montana, not far downstream from Fort Benton, where the Missouri runs green-brown and strong through range country that lifts in great swells to the open horizons. It is brown, featureless, windswept grassland, and the only trees at hand are the scattered cottonwood groves along the river, although we can see the blue bulk of the Bearpaw Mountains rising thirty miles northeast of us, dark with pine.

This is a family affair, as most of our journeys are, with Dycie and our coed daughter Kathy in one freight canoe and seven-year-old Josie and me in the other.

We do not know what to expect and proceed carefully. Our U.S. Geological Survey maps show a few jeep trails above the river, but almost no other roads. There are no towns; the little hamlet of Virgelle is the last clump of civilization until Fort Peck, over two hundred miles downstream. For almost all of that distance, the Missouri is sealed off from the outer world by steepening regions that appear on our maps as dark bands of tightly compressed contour lines—a great maze of deep coulees, ravines, lofty walls, and badlands that stretch for miles on each side of the river. It is a topographic tangle that grows rougher and more complex as we head downstream, and it is apparent that the river is the only smooth, easy route. The maps show shorelines and islands tinged with green—the cottonwood groves that we've learned to welcome. They also indicate the narrows and rapids that we do not welcome, although none has hurt us yet.

This is the new channel of the Upper Missouri, which was diverted southward by the last glacial advance and forced to cut through a plateau whose high points are still marked by the Little Rockies and the Bearpaw and Highwood mountains— small outriders of the Rocky Mountains that we can see whenever we climb the river's headlands. This reach of the Missouri has changed little from one century to the next, for it is confined to a cut that resists change and keeps the river in place. Of all the 2,500 miles of the Missouri River today, the 155 miles between Fort Benton and the head of the Fort Peck Reservoir is the longest unchanged portion still surviving—the old original, still there and still running free and wild.

We carry a portfolio of prints made from the paintings of Karl Bodmer, the Swiss artist who came up here in 1833 with his patron, Prince Maximilian von Wied-Neuwied. He was the first trained artist to see this country and carry its images back downriver, and the landscape has remained faithful to those images. Many of the paintings might have been made last week. Dycie travels with the portfolio at hand and yells over to me, "Look up ahead—see that!", pointing excitedly at her book and then at some towering rock formation or distant cliff.

Bodmer worked furiously in the stretch of river called "The White Rocks Country" or "The Breaks." He and Prince Max were hugely impressed with the rock walls of the Upper Missouri—spectacular stuff after emerging from 2,000 miles of downstream floodplains and prairies, with headlands suddenly looming, the valleys narrowing, and stone walls rising from the river. This was the region where Lewis and Clark had noted: "The river is flowing through a mountain." The middle and lower reaches of the Missouri had few physical features of great interest, but the upper river was a dramatic change and the beginning of what many early travelers had come to see.

For several days we floated and dawdled through a Bodmer gallery, scene for scene. My artist-wife exults in this, commenting on Bodmer's baroque style and comparing the formations now with the formations then. They are still there, wall for wall, spire for spire, as he painted them. We are floating through history as if the river were carrying us back into another time warp, a direct comparison that requires no imagination nor extrapolation. The original scene simply rises before us, and we have a Bodmer print that attests to its authenticity. We put ashore and sit in the same places where Bodmer sat with his sketch-book in that summer of 1833, and note that he tended to foreshorten some of his scenes as if viewing them through a telephoto lens. His vistas have a slight vertical distortion, and lack some of the depth of distance that exists out here. But Dycie brooks no amateur criticism from me; she stoutly defends her hero.

We have drifted below great rocks that towered a hundred feet out of the river, past long galleries of wind-sculptured white stone, through formations pierced with natural windows and crowned with slender towers, by dark igneous dikes from which surrounding materials have weathered away, leaving vertical walls thrust up out of huge hillsides. We stop at some of these places and Kathy and I climb above the river, leaving Dycie with her sketch-pad and Little Jo with the boats. Dry work in this sun and wind, and we've yet to return with any water in the two-quart canteen. We get no sympathy from Dycie; we never give her enough time with Bodmer, it seems.

Most of these rock formations have names. Some are forthright and appropriate, such as Hole-In-The-Wall. But many are the sort of picnicky, anthropocentric labels that have always been stuck on wild America by place-namers whose poverty of taste is exceeded only by poverty of imagination: Cathedral Rock, Citadel Rock, Steamboat Rock, Castle Rock, Chapel Rock.

Prince Max looked at this wildness and saw "pulpits, organs with their pipes, old ruins, fortresses, castles, churches with pointed towers." To him, and to some later visitors, the dramatic impact of the formations was proportional to their resemblance to busted medieval masonry. Perhaps I have a cultural blind spot, but it seems that the ruins of these ancient seabeds—so freely carved by wind and rain—deserve better identities. If they must have names, maybe we should ask a delegation of Black-feet to go in there and do the job right. No one can name a place as well as an Indian.

Our good friend Nels Thoreson of the Montana Fish and Game Department knows this country as well as anyone, and has made cryptic notes on our maps: "pushkin here doubtful," "Pete Balen wrecked," and "was dog town." But the things that catch my eye are the little red circles that simply note: "L&C camp."

Dycie is turned on by Bodner; I'm turned on by L&C. The little red circles leap out of the maps, growing into rings of firelight kindled by Lewis and Clark. We can stop at the places they stopped, build fires where they built theirs, sleep where they slept. This cannot be done downstream where the Missouri has shifted in its floodplain or has been dammed. But our maps indicate the old campsites by day and year—it is possible to locate most with precision, for Lewis and Clark took regular star shots to fix their positions, and their landmarks then were precisely the same as ours now.

By daylight we study Bodmer pictures and their subjects in a three-dimensional history lesson. By firelight we enter a fourth dimension, an eddy in time beside the rolling Missouri, and share camp with the Corps of Discovery.

We were in a grove of cottonwoods in the White Rocks Country, a day's float downstream from the mouth of the Marias.

The wind began rising shortly before midnight, and I left my sleeping bag to check the guy lines of our big cloth fly and examine the moorings of our freight canoes on the gravel bar below camp. The guy lines were in order, and the wind was not chafing the boats against the rock shingle, so I sat on the bow of one and smoked my last cigar.

This is exactly where Lewis and Clark made their May 31, 1805, stop. They had come straining upstream against a river swollen with snowmelt, the men laboring under *la cordelle*—towing their six canoes and two large pirogues with ropes of braided elk leather. The shorelines were soft and muddy that day, and the men had shed their moccasins to gain better traction with bare feet. They were chest-deep in cold water, floundering in shoreline mud or straining barefoot across fields of rocks, the weak towlines often breaking and threatening boats and men. It had been a grueling day, and Lewis noted in his journal: "Their labor is incredibly painful and great, yet these faithful fellows bear it without a murmur . . . at 12 o'clock M. we came to for refreshment and gave the men a dram, which they received with much cheerfulness—and well deserved."

That night they must have eaten their elk meat and rolled into their blankets like dead men, sinking into deep slumber with the young cottonwood leaves ticking in the night above them. Had they snored and muttered as they slept? Was Sacajawea's baby still colicky and fretful—had he cried in the night, and had his mother sung some little Shoshone song?

The night guard at this place would certainly have included a man here at the river with the boats, and he wouldn't have been far from where I sat. What were his night thoughts as he watched the slaty Missouri sliding past? Of home, of St. Louis, or the strange country they were going into? Lewis had seen snowy peaks three days before from a high point thirty miles downstream, and the men knew that they were nearing the gates of the Rockies. And did the mountains concern the river guard as they did his officers?

He would be wearing soggy buckskins, just beginning to draw back into shape after the day's wetting, undried by the cooking fire and now clammy and cold in the midnight wind. The glow from his supper dram of spirits would have faded, leaving him wearier than before, and his thoughts were probably as simple and immediate as any soldier's—was there still some hot coffee at the fire, and how long until he was relieved and could go to his blankets?

Whatever his night thoughts, they did not include me as mine did him, for I was wholly beyond his pale of imagination. Yet, we had something in common. Across the river were the same buttresses of white rock, gleaming faintly in the darkness, and there was the black mass of what later would be called LaBarge Rock. These things we shared, although he would never know it: the same dark river and the same walls of rock, a responsibility for moored boats, and a longing to be back there in the cottonwoods with our sleeping people.

With that thought I stood up to go, and said to the darkness: "My friend, everything will turn out well. You will return safely and be celebrated in schoolbooks." Then, realizing that this assurance would be thin comfort to a private soldier, I added: "By the way, there will be one casualty. On the return trip, Captain Lewis will be accidentally shot in the butt."

From somewhere down the gravel bar there came a faint chuckle. It was the river, of course.

The sweeping scenery of this Upper Missouri is the feature attraction for most visitors, and in itself is enough. But just as impressive to us are certain miniscenes only a few strides across, designed by goblin architects and carved by weather.

Back in Great Falls, Nels Thoreson had tried to tell us about this. Without pinpointing the places (in fact, refusing to do so) he told of delicate sandstone sculptures like cake icing, with balls of wind-carved rock balanced on slender pedestals of stone. It didn't really register then, but it does now.

One day we followed a deep coulee back from the river, hiking up a dry creekbed below rock rims. While Dycie and Kathy and Little Jo prowled the creek searching for exposed bones in the cutbanks, I climbed onto some ledges two hundred feet above them—and blundered into that miniworld of carved sugar.

I stepped around a big pillar and found myself below a field of White Eagle sandstone that rose in distorted waves and splashes up to the ridge crest. It was high here, where the west wind could gain full purchase on the sandstone, working it into fragile traceries and flutings. Nothing was angular; wind and rain had imparted their flowing shapes to the rock, curving the ledges into a wild confusion of scallops, airfoils, smoothed basins, and little fluted vanes. There were two types of sandstone, white and gray, with the gray more resistant to erosion. Here were perfect toadstools with rounded caps of grayish rock perched on delicate stems of white sandstone. There were neat piles of thin round plates split apart by frost action and stacked like large cookies on their short pedestals. It was a thing that would be impressive to Little Jo. Geology means nothing to her—but cookies do. Just beyond was a little half-sphere of gray stone six inches in diameter, also perched on a tee of white rock, and scattered everywhere were circular, fragile wafers of stone that had weathered free of the mother rock.

I had burst upon this place climbing heavily and carelessly, but stopped abruptly. I've known this feeling of clumsiness before, entering a cave room by an underground river and being the first to see its garden of gypsum flowers. The feeling returned as I put my cleated boots onto that white fluting. Now I understood Nels' remark: "I wonder if some of that country back there, if it gets an official stamp of 'scenic river,' might not hurt more from public attention than it would from public neglect." This is what he'd been talking about. It was a place that couldn't survive much traffic. One vandal, in an hour, could undo the work of ages.

I returned with Dycie and the girls, leading them past one of the delicate stonefields, and my artist-bride pronounced it to be the finest free sculpture she had ever seen. We topped the ridge and came onto a flat sheet of white stone that led through scattered cedars across ledges, blocks, and tables. The sculpture here was bolder and on a more massive scale, with the faces of the white ledges sculpted into deep hollows and bold curves.

To our right the ridge fell off into a maze of carved benches and pillars, and at eye level were the tips of large spruces that rose out of pockets in the ravine a hundred feet below. The place is invisible from the river or from the main coulee but might be easily seen by anyone coming by jeep or horse. All in all, a spectacular location for the kind of summer home development that Nels Thoreson dreads.

There were no signs of human traffic, but we hadn't been the first ones here. Something glinted from beside a ledge below us. Lying half-buried in a bed of white sand was an ancient pint whisky bottle. It had been there long enough to acquire a lavender cast, and at this latitude that takes time. The bottle had been hand-blown into a mold, and we'd never seen one like it. Dycie said that its graceful shape had artistic appeal, and flatly opined that it had been left there by either Karl Bodmer or Charlie Russell.

We saw no other traces of people up there in the high sandstone. The fragile fields of sculpture, like the ridge above them, aren't apparent from the river. And most river travelers take their scenery in grand doses, content with the views of pinnacles, spires, and valley walls seen from below or beyond.

It's just as well; the high sandstone of the Upper Missouri can't afford much close attention. The mindless whim that breaks stalactites or smashes cliff swallow nests could wreak havoc here. It is a place to tread lightly and touch nothing. It will always change, for it is a work of change, but that must be left to the wind.

The crystal headwaters of the Missouri—born at the union of the Gallatin, Jefferson, and Madison—are three hundred miles behind us in the Three Forks country. The river has changed greatly in that distance. Back there it is the color of spruce, sky, and snow; here it is the clear metallic brown of a Hawken rifle barrel. It's a different river, this far down, but just as true and genuine as where it sprang from the snowfields of the Absarokas and Bitterroots. Perhaps even more genuine, for it has lost the look of its parent streams and has begun to be its own river.

This is transition water, with neither the pure clarity of its source nor the rolling clouds of silt that it will have farther on. It already has some of the weight and color of the lower river, but without the thousand-acre sandbars. Most of the exposed bars up here are gravel or cobble, although there are certain sandy shorelines that we're leery of. The other day Kathy sprang out of her boat to haul it up on a narrow beach—and sank thigh-deep into the beach. But it is only at quiet shorelines and eddies that we seem to find quicksand; the main bed of the river is as solid as a floor.

Our maps show frequent rapids. However, we were told that such places are dangerous only to the stern-wheelers for which the river was originally charted. So far, that's right. Most of them are mild riffles that can be easily run in a canoe. We went through the first set of rapids without knowing it—there was only a slight quickening of current and a washboarding of the water. But the runs have grown rougher since the Judith River, and we enter them warily and keep to the main thread of the current. No big problems yet, although we have taken a few solid raps from boulders and ledges that we didn't read soon enough, and our keels have new battle scars in their dead-grass paint. Which is all to the good; it keeps us humble.

Like any uncurried Western scenery, the Upper Missouri must be approached with a pragmatic mind as well as a joyful one. We put a lot of planning into our outfit, for this area is strange to us—and strange rivers must be carefully met.

We are in two small freight canoes (not standard square-sterns) that are fifteen feet long, weigh one hundred twelve pounds each, and have six-horsepower outboard motors. We almost brought double-end canoes instead, much preferring to float a scenic river without power. But on the chance that we might make upstream runs or a downstream dash, we chose to have power whether we used it or not—and it was a good choice.

A standard canoe would have been cranky on this trip. For three days we have bucked heavy winds that give the river a strong chop, and our shoe-keel river canoes would be hard to manage. A better choice would be our keeled lake canoes with their greater lateral resistance to water. As it has turned out, we are happy with the broad-beamed freight canoes and their little outboards. Dycie and Kathy are strong paddlers, but these days of wind would have worn them out—and although my seven-year-old shipmate is good company (she makes up songs as we go), her bow paddling is a mite puny.

It is late summer and the river is very low, and there are countless shoals where the main channel splits, wanders, and rejoins itself. We have often touched bottom even though we draw only six inches of water, and I carefully guard the spare shear pins for our motors. We met a pair of Havre fishermen who had broken six shear pins in two days. But, as one of them put it: "There ain't no excuse for that; we just do a lot of cowboying around and don't pay no attention."

We put in near Virgelle and are taking out a week later at the Robinson Bridge at James Kipp State Recreation Area on Highway 191. From there on, the river grows sluggish at the upper end of the Fort Peck Reservoir and the best scenery will be behind us. We'll have gone about 120 miles. With these outboard motors the same trip could be made in three days, but it would be a shame to do it that fast.

There's only one good take-out between Virgelle and the Robinson Bridge—at Judith Landing, about fifty miles downstream from Virgelle. There are no supplies available anywhere along the river, but there's fresh water at Coal Banks Landing near Virgelle, at the Hole-In-The-Wall campsite about thirty miles downstream from there, and at the Judith River campground.

Campsites have never been a problem, and we've yet to share one with other floaters.

The typical Upper Missouri campsite is a grove of cottonwoods that always appears just about the time you need it. There are often range cattle around these places, and most of the groves are closely grazed and parklike. The cattle are good custodians; without them, some of the groves would be impenetrable thickets of wild rose. We have seen no "Keep Out" signs, although one good campsite had a weathered plank that read:

"Don't leave your good time here. Pack out your trash." There are state campsites at Coal Banks Landing, Hole-In-The-Wall, Slaughter (Arrow) River, Judith Landing, and just upstream from Cow Island. The Hole-In-The-Wall camp is on a big open flat and has three roomy log lean-tos for shelter. It also has a pump where we all took a bucket-bath one chilly evening. The valley is still echoing.

It's country with plenty of elbowroom; we haven't been stifled by crowds. At the Judith River I asked the old ferryman how far it was to the Robinson Bridge take-out.

"Oh, I reckon about seventy miles," he said.

"Any ranches or people along the river?"

"Well, about thirteen miles down there's another ferry, but nobody's there. About twenty-eight miles down there's a little ranch. That's about it."

"How about ranches above the river, up on top?"

"Don't count on that," he said. "There's some big spreads up there, but folks are a little sparser out to the sides than they are on the main steam . . ."

All in all, a floatable river—which isn't the usual thing in the West. It can be safely handled by a family with an adequate outfit, with no worry about wild, heavy rapids or unusual hazards. Still, it's a big river and any big river demands respect. The kids must wear life preservers, and that isn't a bad idea for grownups, either. As far as risk is concerned—well, we wouldn't hesitate to take Little Jo on this trip again. But as on any jaunt into remote country, a small child must do what he's told and do it at once without sass.

Plan well, be alert, and have fun. As the old cowboy said: "Keep a leg on each side and your head in the middle—and don't fall on your guitar hand!"

The river is a magnet, pulling birds from the sky and animals in from the high plains on every side.

We are surprised at the number of Canada geese this region produces; we often drift around bends and sweep down on family flocks that are less impressed with the encounters than we are. Ten years ago an aerial survey between Fort Benton and Robinson Bridge showed 270 nesting geese, and we doubt if there's been any decline.

There are frequent flocks of shorebirds at work on the wet margins of gravel bars; we rarely take time to identify them though, for the gravel spits are often just above or below rapids that give us other things to think about.

We are constantly attended by great blue herons that escort us downriver, driving steadily along in majestic slow motion and alighting in shallows ahead to wait for us—letting down with the odd disassembling process that landing herons have, like camp chairs being opened up. There are some early flights of teal that may be staging for migration, and two days ago I jumped a half-dozen cinnamon teal that glowed in the early sun like newly smelted Montana copper.

In the Haystack Butte area above the White Rocks, the riverside cliffs are studded with swallow nests. We have seen a couple of prairie falcons and three golden eagles—all in the badlands below the mouth of the Judith. It seems to us that these badlands hold more wildlife than does the White Rocks Country upriver. This becomes more apparent as we near the end of our float and approach the million-acre Charles M. Russell National Wildlife Range.

Today Dycie and Kathy came around a bend and startled several elk in the shallows; they foamed up out of the water and took the steep cutbank easily, running off across the flat with the effortless grace of fine quarterhorses. In the riverside timber, and on the brushy islands, there are white-tailed deer all the way up to Fort Benton. I doubt if local hunters have much effect on these deer—many Montana hunters regard the whitetail as a strange kind of Eastern bug. This is mainly mule deer range, and game biologists estimate that the Upper Missouri's breaks hold an average of at least seven mule deer per square mile. Which isn't very high density compared to other mule deer ranges, but it may be made up for by quality of individuals. Yesterday, while walking up a deep coulee, we flushed the biggest mulie doe we have ever seen. She paused fifty yards away to look us over, her yellowish-bay coat sleek and bright with summer.

I wish I'd brought my rabbit-squaller to toll up a few bobcats and coyotes. This country is full of them. Several times we've seen cat tracks along the water's edge, and each night we hear the song-dogs. Every cottonwood grove has its resident great horned owls. Resident beaver, too. Our prime source of firewood is cottonwoods girdled by beaver and felled by wind.

The cast of characters has gaps, of course. The headlands above the river once abounded with bighorn sheep, groves along the river held grizzlies, and the open bottomland flats teemed with elk, pronghorns, and bison. Those flats must have been constantly occupied by someone or other—with encampments of Indians one month and herds of bison the next. Early river travelers were often in sight of buffalo for weeks at a time—a most welcome thing, not only for the meat provided but because peaceful herds meant decamped Indians. Still, even peaceful buffalo have their moments. Just below the mouth of the Judith, Lewis and Clark were visited by a lone bull that came storming up out of the river at night, climbed over one of the pirogues, and charged off through the center of their camp.

Not far upstream from there, they came upon a great "push-kin," or buffalo jump, where a herd of bison had been driven off an escarpment by Indians. "A vast many mangled carcasses" covered the river's edge at the foot of the cliff a few miles downstream from the creek that the explorers would name "Slaughter River." We've heard that beneath some of these riverside cliffs it is possible to dig trenches through layers of old buffalo bones—sites of pushkins thousands of years old.

We nooned near one of these places, beaching the canoes in an overpowering wind. I picked up a round sphere of gray sandstone that had weathered out of the cliff and presented it proudly to my wife. For years, and for reasons known only to her, she has wanted a perfect stone baseball. But a few minutes later Kathy found an even better one, and then Dycie topped us both by finding the heavy femur of a long-dead bison, partly mineralized and stained brown with oxides.

Standing under the face of that steep headland, I tried to imagine how it had looked with a bellowing tide of huge animals pouring over its edge—a roaring surge of hundreds of tons of flesh and bone plunging into death through a vast pall of dust. Sometimes these debacles were caused by lone men—the buffalo-leaders, the tribe-feeders, chosen of all hunters, with hearts as strong as *Hohost* the grizzly's and legs as swift as *Ahtik* the antelope's. Naked under his full buffalo robe, such a man would draw the attention of a herd being hazed toward the breaks by his comrades. Seeing him, the buffalo might follow. He would lead them over the cliff-edge, running for his life and hoping to reach the sheltering crevice or rock overhang before it was engulfed by stampede. If he won, he would strut full-bellied at the fire that night, reciting his deeds and singing of courage and skill. But how often had he lost? How many hunter bones were mingled with the bison bones under our feet?

A chancy living, back in those times before the strange and wonderful "dog-elk" had come up from the south to be trained as a buffalo horse.

Our last night out. We have pitched the canoe fly just up from the river's edge, for the grove behind us is thick with wild rose. Dycie, wise in such things, noted the growing silences that always come as we near the end of another trip, and injected our sagging morale with an English plum pudding. It may be the first plum pudding ever eaten on Cow Island, but I wouldn't bet on that. Anything could have happened at this place.

As usual, we are deep in history. This was a famous landing for deep-draft steamboats that could go no farther upstream during low water and discharged cargoes here to be lightered upriver in mackinaw boats. It was also a favorite ford for Indians, and Chief Joseph arrived with his Nez Percé in late September, 1877—still hurting from a bad fight with the Crows and with General Oliver Howard in pursuit.

The steamer *Benton* had unloaded fifty tons of freight on Cow Island and headed back downriver, leaving a small mountain of supplies guarded by a sergeant, twelve soldiers, and four civilians. Although the Nez Percé band consisted largely of worn, tired families, it included a hundred seasoned warriors who were superbly mounted. The seventeen white men prudently retired to rifle pits on the north side of the river where they had a clear field of fire toward the Cow Island ford. While a few warriors watched the soldiers, the rest of the band looted the unguarded supplies—rejoicing in the windfall of food and equipment. Shooting did not break out until early evening; in the failing light there were no losses on either side. The Indians set fire to the remaining supplies, headed north, and a few days later Colonel Clendennin at Fort Benton received a message:

"Colonel: Chief Joseph is here and says he will surrender for two hundred bags of sugar. I told him to surrender without the sugar. He took the sugar and will not surrender. What will I do?—Michael Foley."

It was a brief last victory for the Nez Percé. Colonel Nelson Miles was on his way from the east and would find them at Snake Creek in early October. And although the troops were badly bloodied, with some units losing over half their strength, the odds finally told. Chief Joseph had fought his last fight, and the long retreat had ended.

But the colors fade slowly. The ford is still there, shallow and firm, and if you know where to look you can still see traces of the rifle pits. We sat in our dusk and looked north into that other dusk when white-rumped Appaloosa ponies splashed across the ford toward the entrenched riflemen and the thudding Springfields, leaving Cow Island lit with the flames of burning supplies.

Then Kathy saw a moving V in the center of the river. The V resolved into a very large beaver that was joined by a buddy from the far bank, and as Kathy stood for a better look, both dived. There were no sharp tail-slaps of alarm. There seldom are. The sounds were like a pair of ten-pound boulders being dropped into deep water with a massive *plunk*.

The beavers soon surfaced again, and a hundred yards upstream three others came out on a flat to graze—blanket-grade beavers that looked like small bears in the deepening twilight. There were three on the flat and at least four more swimming in front of camp, and they were still there when it was too dark to see. When the video ended, the audio began. There was the occasional beaver splash, a pair of owls opened up in the trees behind us, and a squad of coyotes began tuning up on the high ground across the river. The night shift was coming on, and making no secret of it.

Sometime deep in the night I sat up in my sleeping bag to adjust the old canvas coat that I wad up for a pillow, clearing my throat as I did so, and there was a boulder-plunk in the river forty feet away. This registered, in a dim way, as the proper thing. The circle had closed. What had begun with beaver, and led to beaver passing, was ending with beaver returned. Colter and Bird Woman were gone with Lewis and Clark, the chiefs had passed beyond the perfidy of white cavalry, the steamboats were wrecked and rotted, we were heading home to St. Louis as so many other travelers of the Upper Missouri had done, but the beaver endure. The river still belongs to beaver, I thought, and that fits in with river unchanging and coyotes still singing and the same stars above.

I almost had a grip on some profound observation, but it slipped away and I was asleep.

The High Beyond

THIS MOUNTAIN COUNTRY EXPANDS AND INTENSIFIES many things that men love and dread in the outdoors. It's a land of heroic exaggeration where you can breathe more and get less air, walk farther and make less distance, take a quicker bath, have more sudden weather, and spit farther than anywhere else in North America. The old trappers said that "meat don't spile" in the high country. Packers claim that some of their country is "so cussed tall that you got to lay down on your back and look up twice to see the top of it." Bud Hurd told us of a friend who rode around a northern Colorado mountain alone, and "when he come back ten days later, neither him or his horse had shoes!"

There are many other fine places, and they are all genuine places and good for men to be in, whether they are stormy coasts, plains, canoe rivers, redwood groves, or just the squirrel woods of home.

But always, standing apart from the ordinary places, its prodigious horizons crowding the vault of heaven, there is the high country. It will always be there to lift men's eyes, outlasting the

prairies and the redwoods—outlasting men, and the eroding
lichens, and even life itself.

The alpine fastness perplexes most men, and they cannot
decide if it is a good thing or not. It has few of the common
advantages of other places, and a multitude of disadvantages
that are unique. Some people actively dislike the strange world
that lies above 8,000 feet, and will never enter it. Maybe they
secretly fear that they will fall from the high places, and so they
stay in their valleys. And maybe this valley way of thinking is
best, for it meets our modern needs for comfort, crowds, and
safety from falling.

Yet, there are things that the valleys cannot give us. Such as
the high notes of an elk's bugling, drifting down to the spike
camp through three miles of perfect air. Such as a pika whistling
and spreading his hay on sunlit talus, and Swede's spurs jingling
toward the picket line at dawn, and the thin, wild wind.

And if a man is to keep safe from falling, he can never aspire
to hunt toward some incredible height and stand there alone,
and consider the smallness of valleys, and how far they lie
beneath him.

Part III

OLD FRIENDS

Sudden upon the elm-tree tops the crow
Unceremonious visit pays and croaks,
Then swoops away. From mossy barn the owl
Bobs hasty out—wheels round and, scared as soon,
As Hastily retires.The ducks grow wild ...

John Clare

Giants in the Cliffs

IT BEGINS, SAY, ABOUT A HUNDRED MILES UPSTREAM from St. Louis, high in a limestone wall that rises two hundred feet above the rolling Missouri.

There is a low crevice that extends several yards back into the cliff. Under the rock overhang, out of the weather, a shallow crater in the dirt floor is lined with small sticks and grass, and the starburst down feathers that a Canada goose has plucked from her belly. Yesterday there were four eggs in the nest. Today there are four olive-yellow goslings on the ledge, milling about their mother.

The gander is just beyond, swinging out over the river on short flights and returning to call and coax, stirring his mate and the goslings, urging them to leave the cliff and join him. He is not to be ignored. He is a majestic bird, a *Branta canadensis maxima*, greatest of the subspecies of Canada geese, spanning over six feet across the wings and weighing as much as eighteen pounds—among our waterfowl, second in size only to the wild swans.

127

The goose leaves the nest ledge to join him, circling and hovering a few yards away and adding to her mate's clamor and the rising excitement of the goslings, calling to them with a low and urgent *kum! kum! kum!* The day-old goslings are at the brink of the ledge, and now they launch themselves one at a time toward their noisy parents, but with slightly different results. They fall free, plunging over a hundred feet to the shattered rocks at the base of the cliff.

That the goslings are not killed nor badly injured is a small miracle. They are not wood duck nestlings, after all—weightless little balls of fluff that pop out of a nesting snag and fall twenty feet onto earth or water. These are *maxima* goslings that may weigh a hundred grams or more, and they fall forty yards to talus rock. Sometimes, perhaps, the impact is broken by brush growing on the lower slope. But in any manner it is a harsh way to enter the real world, striking on the cruel rocks and rolling and struggling down the jumble of talus to the base of the slope where their parents are waiting.

And then, another hazard. Between the bank of the river and the base of the cliff is a railroad track. To the goslings, the line of track represents two steel walls between them and the water—a pair of railroad rails only seven inches high, but flanged, over-hung and slippery, a major barrier to the tiny geese. Even if there is a small gap between the rail and the rock ballast of the roadbed, the goslings are likely to be oblivious to a possibility that lies below their eye level. Unable to climb over the rails, and unable to comprehend chances to squeeze under them, the little brood must struggle down the roadbed until a crossing can be found.

This is an acutely dangerous time. The brood is fully exposed, in daylight and in the open, in a narrow travel lane between cliff and riverbank that is under the constant scrutiny of furred and feathered hunters. But the goslings have a formidable escort. It may be the goose that leads them, with the gander bringing up the rear, and the old birds are in no mood to be trifled with. Geese in the spring are never sweet-tempered. A nesting Canada goose has been known to knock a horseman out of the saddle and break his arm. And in a situation like this, with the old birds trying desperately to lead their brood to life-giving water, any interference would be savagely resented. A ten-pound red fox would find little profit in tackling thirty pounds of enraged wild geese.

Two hundred yards down the track, with the goslings struggling along over the crushed rock of the ballast, the family comes to a small trestle that passes over a creek. The problem of the railroad rails has been solved, and the goslings follow their parents down the steep bank and enter water for the first time. From there it is only thirty yards to the river—and more danger.

The geese must reach a willow-grown island and its quiet backwater on the other side of the river. To do so requires the day-old goslings to cross the main thread of the Missouri River's spring current, and between the sheltered mouth of the creek and the opposite shore there is a quarter-mile of powerful river. In crossing, the goslings will be swept far downstream and will surely touch at a barren and inhospitable section of riverbank. Having survived the plunge from the cliff, the deadly journey along the exposed railbed, and the exhausting swim across the Missouri's channel, they must then travel a mile or more back up the riverbank—much of it along open levees—to reach the haven of sheltering willows and quiet backwaters. Still, they were lucky. Their nesting cliff was almost directly across the river from a brood area. There are other nesting cliffs from which the goslings must travel many miles to suitable brood havens, with what must be only a thread of a chance of succeeding.

How many goslings attempt these incredible odysseys from cliff nests to distant brood areas? How many survive? We don't know the answers; it was only yesterday that we knew the questions.

The giant Canada geese that nest in the dolomite cliffs of the Missouri River between St. Charles and Jefferson City, Missouri, were long unknown to naturalists. Although geese were sometimes seen along the river in late spring and summer, and known to be rearing broods on certain river islands and backwaters, there was no reason to feel that the birds weren't also nesting there.

For about twenty years, however, there had been vague rumors of Canada geese actually nesting in the cliffs of the Missouri. The rumors were never confirmed, but they were strangely persistent, and in the spring of 1971 a farmer near Hermann, Missouri, reported cliff-nesting geese. His report was investigated by Missouri Department of Conservation biologists Charles Schwartz and Glenn Chambers. Charlie and Glenn found and photographed geese nesting in the bluffs near Hermann—thereby answering the big question and raising a hundred smaller ones.

To University of Missouri graduate student David Graber, who would begin research on the geese nesting in a hundred miles of river cliffs, the key questions were: where did the flock originate, how large was it, and what were its habits?

At first, it was generally assumed that these cliff-nesters might be birds that had broken away from the resident goose flock at the Busch Memorial Wildlife Area near St. Charles. That flock had been established in the early 1950s, at about the time when rumors of cliff-nesters had begun. Besides, the Busch Wildlife Area birds were western Canada geese of the same subspecies that sometimes nest in cliffs above such western rivers as the Snake and the Salmon.

However, there were snags in these pat assumptions. For one thing, Missouri game biologists and rivermen had been seeing geese in the vicinity of the nesting cliffs since at least the 1930s—long before any captive flocks had been established downriver. Furthermore, Dave Graber found that the cliff-nesters were really *maxima*, the giant Canada goose of the subspecies that originally nested in Missouri. There is a distinct possibility that the big geese have always nested in the Missouri River cliffs, even after the nesting of Canada geese had generally ceased in Missouri sometime around the turn of the century.

But if such cliff-nesting is an established practice, why wasn't it detected and described much earlier? Well, why should it have been? Although the geese were commonly seen in the vicinity of the cliffs, and perhaps even alighting on certain high ledges, what reason was there to think that they were actually nesting up there? Few, if any, of the cliff nests can be seen by man from above, below, or from either side. They are most easily visible from rather close range, straight out from the cliffs. And even so, they are often associated with small bushes or rocks that help conceal them.

Besides, there just aren't all that many nests. Of the thirty-two nests that Graber has found along his hundred-mile study area, only nineteen are actual bluff nests and the rest are ground nests above or below the cliffs. The cliff nests were on ledges from thirty to 150 feet above the ground; to inspect them, the young researcher rappelled down from the tops of the cliffs.

Charlie Schwartz has made several flights by helicopter from below Hermann to Jefferson City, keeping about fifty yards away from the river cliffs and observing and taking pictures. He has flushed fourteen pairs of geese from one choice mile of cliffs—but could see only three nests there. That was in late April and early May, when those paired geese very possibly meant fourteen nests. And if an experienced field biologist sees only one-fifth of the nests that are probably there, even though he is in the best position to see them, such cliff nests must be virtually impossible for the casual observer to find.

These dolomite cliffs are vertical faces of split, fissured limestone that may be two hundred feet high—rugged steeps with deep horizontal crevices and ledges defining the ancient strata, often crumbling and rotten, the sort of stuff that isn't safe to negotiate except perhaps by rope, from above, and always chancy at best. Some of the nest sites are on abrupt grassy terraces that are parts of major ledge systems. Other geese nest at the upper rim of the cliffs in clumps of cedar, and on grassy cedar-grown outcroppings just under the main rim. There are also isolated nest crevices that are surely inaccessible to anything but birds, and are almost as safe from wild hunters as from men—small overhung shelves and crevices in blank faces of stone with no access ledges or approaches of any kind.

During his helicopter flights, Charlie saw foxes running along ledges and narrow faults. They seemed at home up there on the cliff faces among the crevices and shelving overhangs, and if there are red and gray foxes haunting those cliffs, there are surely raccoons, bobcats, hawks, and owls. A special community that is utterly inaccessible to man and his works, and you don't find many of those. Many of the goose nests, of course, are accessible to predators. But even if an enterprising, sure-footed 'coon or gray fox should penetrate the sheer defenses of a cliff nest, there's a distinct possibility that he'd be batted out into deep center field. A blind, narrow ledge high in a sheer cliff is no place to provoke a pair of nesting geese.

It was to be something of a surprise party.

Our good friends Libby and Charlie Schwartz were about to receive honorary DSc degrees from the University of Missouri, and my wife Dycie and I were saluting them with a field lunch to end all field lunches. Which doesn't have much to do with the subject at hand, except that lunch was in a bankside thicket near a nesting cliff, and the geese were there.

We stopped at noon near the west end of a line of cliffs, stepped off the railroad track into the trees, and shed our packs. To the general approval, my old rucksack produced a bottle of chilled champagne, two quarts of fresh strawberries, and whipped cream. Then, with a flourish, Libby topped that with a loaf of her fresh nutbread and two cold smoked mallards. Our table was a handhewn oak railroad tie, and it may have been the first time that French champagne has ever been splashed into goblets in a Missouri hobo jungle, complementing smoked duck and off-season strawberries. I've said it before and I'll say it again: there's a helluva lot more to birdwatching than birdwatching.

All during lunch we had been seeing a half-dozen Canada geese paddling in and out of a backwater chute across the river, and loafing on sandbars and the end of a pile dike. Charlie opined that they were probably ganders, with geese on the nests in the cliffs, and this was verified almost at once when two of the birds picked up and flew across the river to the cliffs just east of us. One vanished into a towering face of rock about a quarter-mile away; the other flew directly into a rocky crevice no more than two hundred yards from us. He landed on a ledge, turned and settled himself, and we caught a glimpse of the goose raising her head behind him. The nest crevice was not very deep or wide, and the gander was unable to join his mate farther back under the overhang. As we stood to adjust the spotting scope, the big gander flattened and froze. He could still be seen—but only because we knew where to look.

After a while we took a post-prandial stroll over that way, walking directly beneath the nest crevice. It was about fifty feet above the talus slope at the base of the cliff, and the gander's head was now thrust over the edge, motionless and watchful, neck flattened against the rock. We eyeballed each other at less than thirty yards for ten minutes—and even with 10X binoculars I could detect no sign of movement.

At the end of a pile dike, about two hundred yards away, stood another pair of Canadas. Even at that distance, the difference between them was striking. The nearer bird was a common Canada goose, possibly weighing nine pounds and of conventional goose dimensions. It was dwarfed by its companion, which appeared to be at least one-fourth larger, a huge bird whose rather long, swannish neck had a powerful and somewhat thickened quality. This gander was standing extremely erect, long neck perfectly vertical. He seemed to be somewhat paler than his companion, and through the scope we could see the massive bill and odd rearward hook of the upper part of the white cheek patch that so often brands the *maxima*. It was the fabled "real goose hisse'f" that I've heard old Missouri River hunters tell about. To my everlasting regret, I remember chaffing friends like Ralph "Bogie" Jones of Onawa, Iowa, when he told about shooting eighteen-pound honkers in the old wild-river days. And me, in my newly conferred university wisdom, scoffing at the old hunter yarns of eighteen-pound honkers, denying that they existed and saying that if they ever had it must have been a long time ago, back in the days of hoop snakes and wampus cats.

Still, there were some scholars who believed that a giant

Canada goose had existed, even though it may have been extinct for decades. In 1951 Jean Delacour, working from extensive notes left by the late James Moffitt, grasped the nettle and named this semi-legendary bird *Branta canadensis maxima*. But Delacour himself, in 1954, said: "The giant Canada goose appears to be extinct." H. Albert Hochbaum, one of North America's premier waterfowl biologists, added in 1955 that: "The giant Canada goose, which Delacour and Moffitt considered a distinct subspecies, is forever gone from the Mississippi Valley."

Nearly everyone in the wildlife profession would have agreed with Al—and many doubted there had ever been a giant goose at all. Small wonder that so many experts were crestfallen (although wild with interest) when Harold Hanson of the Illinois Natural History Survey astounded wildlifers and ornithologists in 1962 by officially rediscovering the giant Canada goose—in the city lake of Rochester, Minnesota! Hanson's brilliant study of the giant Canada not only firmly established its existence and supported the old hunter yarns of huge honkers that topped eighteen pounds, but found that there are at least 55,000 of these geese in existence. Our largest wild goose is not only with us, but in numbers.

Should it really be surprising, then, that we were unaware of the Missouri River's cliff-nesting geese until the last few years? We had trouble enough just seeing a giant wild goose that was under our noses. Who'd have believed that it would behave like a cliff swallow?

The nesting sites in the stone cliffs are secure and unchanging. But no nesting site can be any better than the brood habitat that augments it.

After leaving the nest, goslings must have water and escape cover, security and food. In Missouri River terms, this means sandbar islands with some grass and trees, and backwater chutes and sloughs that separate mainland from island, and perhaps oxbow lakes where the river has cut across the necks of great bends, isolating the meandered channel and forming crescent-shaped ponds. Quiet water, and quiet, secure places for goslings to feed and loaf and grow. But although the nesting cliffs extend intermittently for a hundred miles in east-central Missouri, offering a multitude of potential nesting sites, quality brood-rearing areas are few and becoming fewer. Between Jefferson City and St. Charles, Dave Graber found only five of these prime brood-rearing areas. He noted that while such areas were near nesting areas, not all nesting areas were near brood-rearing areas—and some newly hatched goslings were as far as twenty miles from suitable brood habitat. The tiny goslings are capable of extended and arduous journeys; despite their delicate, toylike appearance, they are amazingly tough. But how many can manage twenty-mile journeys through hostile countryside?

There was a time when Canada geese nested in large numbers along Missouri's portion of the Big Muddy, and trumpeter and whistling swans may have nested there, too. The river was wild then, a strong brown giant that built and wrecked incessantly, sealing off oxbow lakes, raising sandbars in one place and delving deep scour-holes in another, throwing itself into wild bends that embraced great sandbars with their "willow slaps" and peaceful chutes and back-sloughs—constructing islands that were miles long, their willowed crests alternating with broad sandflats and inch-deep ponds that teemed with plovers, curlews, cranes, and egrets. Along wild shorelines overhung with immense and ancient trees, the pale-barked upper decks of the sycamores were ablaze with the red-yellow-and-green Carolina parakeets. And in spring and fall during the Grand Passage of the waterfowl, the old market hunters would say that the high bars and backwaters were "black-full of poultry."

The federal government helped put a stop to such nonsense. All those bends and islands and split channels were interfering with commerce. The old Missouri River Commission set to work in 1884, and the U.S. Army Corps of Engineers took over in 1902. The effects on the fish and wildlife resources of the Missouri River have been catastrophic.

In 1879, Missouri's portion of the Missouri River was 544 miles from the extreme southeastern corner of Nebraska to the mouth of the river near St. Louis. In 1972 the same stretch of Missouri River was 498.4 miles long—a net loss of 45.6 river miles. Great bends and meanders had been eliminated, and the river was being transformed into a deep, fast, narrow chute.

Also in 1879, the Missouri River's total water surface area in Missouri had been 121,739 acres. By 1954 this had shrunk to 71, 151 acres—a loss of 50,588 acres. Since then, an additional 10,000 acres of water area have been lost. The total river area has been reduced by half!

This was partly the result of straightening, but much of that lost water area has resulted from pile dikes—long lines of heavy wooden piles filled and buttressed with broken rock, extending far out into the river and deflecting the current toward the center of the channel. When such dikes are built across chutes or sloughs that separate large islands from the mainland, the backwaters quickly fill with silt. Thus connected to the shore, the islands are usually cleared and put into cultivation. From 1879 to 1954, the surface area of Missouri River islands in the state was reduced from 24,419 acres to only 419 acres—a reduction of 98 percent.

However, the fact that the wild islands were vanishing and the river was narrowing did not mean that there were widened bankside zones of public wildlife habitat. Although the Missouri River is supposed to be public domain from bank to bank, and although public funds are used to narrow the channel, the portions of floodplain that were formerly in public ownership do not continue to be. Such lands are almost always annexed by riparian landowners, and nearly 67,000 acres of land that formerly lay in the Missouri River's main channel have been lost to the public domain in the state of Missouri alone.

This shrinkage of the Missouri River's total water and channel areas is a direct and unmitigable loss to wildlife. The river's lost water surface, for example, is more than *five times* greater than the total water area that has been provided by Swan Lake National Wildlife Refuge, Squaw Creek National Wildlife Refuge, Fountain Grove Public Hunting Area, and August A. Busch Memorial Wildlife Area, and the Trimble Wildlife Area—all of which are adjacent to the Missouri River or not far from it. A rich and varied corridor of wildlife habitat has been methodically reduced to a sterile sluiceway, its wild margins wrested from the public domain by the Army Corps of Engineers and a few riparian landowners.

Considering all this, it seems a minor miracle that one of the best things has survived almost to the last—and that the cliff-nesting geese of the Missouri River have managed to cling to a tradition that is so incredibly fragile. That tradition only germinates in the heights of the dolomite cliffs—it is fanned and nurtured in the brood areas of the river, those half-dozen sand-bar-and-backwater nurseries in which the goslings reach flight size and adulthood.

The question, of course, is whether the Corps of Engineers will let the geese keep the last scraps of wild river. It's a rhetorical question. We know the answer.

The Dance
on Monkey Mountain

ON MY EDGE OF THE PAVEMENT a road-killed fox was being attended by a pair of crows. There was oncoming traffic and I was unable to swerve, and the wheels of the car passed within inches of the defunct Reynard. The crows calmly gauged my approach as they always do, floated up into the air as I passed under them, and dropped back down to their dinner. They had calculated my brake horsepower and closing speed with the acuity of an Indianapolis pit crew.

They were in character, polishing off an adult red fox that had been unable to coexist with traffic. A red fox is pretty handy at coexisting with almost anything, but he's not as handy at it as the common crow. Few critters are.

In thirty years of tooling along country roads, I have seen many sly creatures that had been, clobbered by cars: mink, coyotes, red fox, gray fox, white-tailed deer, bobcats, and even one lightning rod salesman. Plus a multitude of poor little goofs that never seem to adjust to traffic: a host of songbirds, sparrow hawks, cottontails, ground squirrels, and garter snakes. But never a crow. I've yet to see a crow that had been hit by a car. Crows have a natural immunity to traffic, and experience gives them booster shots. Call it adaptability, or skilled judgement in familiar feeding situations. But it's more likely a deep and abiding case of the smarts.

If the common crow isn't the endpoint of current avian evolution, he can't be far from it. Sleek, hard-feathered, adaptable, and superbly generalized, he's a bird for all seasons. It's as if the most practical, general features of the class Aves had been built into one bird, plus a low sense of humor and a raffish cleverness that is disturbingly familiar. Most birds behave like birds, endearing themselves to us as a flash of color, a burst of song, or a high, aloof vigilance. But crows may remind us of us—something that's hard to forgive.

I like crows.

Oh, I've hunted them often enough, but this was never attended by any rancor and it always reinforced liking with respect. To hunt crows is part of an acquaintance process, and reveals many facets of crow character. To be mobbed by a raging gang of black banditti teaches one thing; stalking a lone sentinel teaches another. Like men, crows may yield to mob madness and commit insane indiscretions that range from mayhem to heroism, and within the hour they return to being keen, perceptive master of themselves and their world. The common crow is an animal of many parts that may be more clearly revealed to an ardent predator than a casual observer.

My bond with crows began long ago during certain bitter winter evenings when we traveled together. For several winters at the tail of the Depression I market-hunted rabbits in central Iowa—a grueling enterprise that resulted in a lot more seasoning then revenue. Among other things, it taught me that it's a little easier to be famished and weary if you're not alone. And when I'd turn homeward at day's end and face the miles of crusted snow that lay between me and supper, there were usually a few crows for company—seeming just as tired and hungry as I was. They would escort me in little tattered flocks, beating patiently into the bitter wind, going home. The lights that were beginning to glow in the windows of distant farmhouses were not for us. We belonged to no one but ourselves and to the bleak world whose graying land faded into grayer sky as evening came on, where nothing moved but a few wind-buffeted crows and a boy stumbling through the iron twilight.

Most other birds had gone south; indeed, so had most crows. Those that escorted me were the toughest of a tough breed—friendless and persecuted with every man's hand turned against them, gleaning a hard living from a hard land. Like me, they had spent the day searching for the Main Chance—and like me, they probably hadn't found it. We were hunters and scroungers fallen on hard times together, heading for our home roosts after a day of deficit spending. Those crows didn't have much and neither did I—but for a little while there we had each other to divert our attention and ease the last long miles to home.

When bluebirds and swallows return, I will always welcome them with relief and affection—but never with the respect that I hold for the crows that never went.

Some general comments on a general bird:

Crows are members of the clan *Corvidae*, of course, a tribe that includes all manner of scamps: the jays, jackdaws, rooks, magpies, and ravens. The common crow's full name, *Corvus brachyrhynchos*, may not flow off the tongue as do some scientific names, but it somehow fits the owner. Next time you hit your thumb with a hammer, try saying it fast several times. It's good substitute profanity and doesn't corrupt listening kids.

Spanning twenty-four inches across his slaty wings, with a total body length of about twenty inches, the crow is probably our largest generalized bird. Most other birds his size are somehow specialized in structure and function, but the crow is simply an outsized songbird. His powerful beak is adapted to picking and pecking, and is as useful in predation and carrion-feeding as in field-gleaning. Almost anything that's edible—from seed to grub to nestling—can be crow provender. What with one thing or another, the common crow has the physical and psychological equipment to exploit almost any possibility that comes along.

One day last summer I drove through Greenwich, Connecticut, heading for LaGuardia Airport and the flight home. There was a big new office building in downtown Greenwich, and while pausing at a stoplight I happened to glance up at the roof. Far above the street at the edge of a lofty cornice was perched a lone crow. He was calmly surveying the confusion below, wondering how he could put it to use and looking as self-possessed as if he'd been in a Kansas cottonwood.

I caught my plane and returned to St. Louis, bailed my old truck out of the parking lot, and headed for Illinois. Naturally, I hit Lindbergh Boulevard just in time to be ingested by the 4:30 traffic. And as I inched along, I happened to catch a whirl of motion above a small tree in a nearby factory area. A lone crow was being harassed by a small gray bird, and as they flew over the traffic jam just ahead, I could see that the crow held an egg in his beak. Twice in the same day, a thousand miles apart, I'd seen crows busy being crows in heavily urbanized situations.

It wasn't surprising. I've often seen crows in untidy downtown shopping centers at dawn, checking litter and debris. They commonly haunt manicured suburbs at first light (not usually making much noise about it), and I've seen them strolling across lawns on Chicago's near North Side only a few miles from the Loop. By full daylight, they're gone.

Yet, crows are basically farmland birds with a yen for landscapes that mix trees, cultivated fields, feedlots, and pastures. They are rarely seen in real wilderness, where corvids are likely to be represented by ravens and jays.

Old settlers in the midwestern states claimed that crows were rare on the early prairies, even along the breaks of the Missouri River. Crows apparently arrived in eastern Nebraska in the early 1860s, exploiting changes that were beginning to evict the indigenous magpies and ravens. The common crow flourished with the advent of prairie farming and the planting of windbreaks and tree claims; in the East, much the same effect was achieved as the vast expanses of original forest were opened by settlers.

If it's true that there are more crows today than at the time of Columbus, then the golden age of crowdom must have been in the waning years of the nineteenth century when American farmland as a whole possessed the somewhat ragged quality that Crow seems to dote on. It was a time of small family farms, diverse grain and livestock production, with young tree claims maturing on the prairies and remnants of original forest still surviving in the East.

Crow moved into the new situations with the raffish abandon of a pickpocket at a Republican convention. Man cleared and toiled; Crow jeered and foiled. The black brigands committed outrageous acts of disrespect and got away with it, moving the Reverend Henry Ward Beecher to reflect: "If men had wings and bore black feathers, few of them would be clever enough to be crows." Their brazen affronts to the American farmer are pretty well typified by the two Florida crows that were once seen perched on a cow's back. It was February, when Florida crows are scrounging nest materials, and each of the birds had a beakful of white hairs that had been plucked from the back of the cow.

That cow probably wasn't flattered by the crows' attention, but it could have been worse. In areas of crow concentrations in Kansas, there are reports from angry farmers that newborn calves are being blinded and even killed by crows. At the same time, there are complaints of heavy damage to milo and winter wheat.

Some depredations of crows, however, may be more apparent than real. Although corn is claimed to be the favorite food of crows, a study conducted in five New York counties indicated that corn was less than fourteen percent of the crow's annual food—and most of that was taken during winter. In May, when corn is sown in central New York, it amounted to only one percent of the diet of crows studied. Other work has shown that confined crows preferred live mealworms to all other foods offered (including grain), which supports one biologist's finding that a single family of crows may account for 40,000 grubs, caterpillars, army worms, and other insects during the nesting season alone.

In my field of game management, Crow has long been regarded as a prime spoiler—especially of waterfowl and pheasants.

There's no doubt that crows will watch the movements of adult ducks, and if an incubating duck is flushed within sight of crows, they can easily find her eggs. Even though the duck covers eggs before leaving her nest to feed, this may not help if crows see her take off. It has been noted that duck nests with good concealment (by human standards) may be destroyed just as readily as exposed ones—in fact, the better-hidden nests may even suffer the most crow damage. On one marsh area, only four ducklings hatched from two hundred eggs. Crows got the rest. Of over five hundred duck nests once studied in the prairie provinces of Canada, about half were destroyed before hatching. The crow led the list of predators, taking thirty-one percent of the nests.

But in spite of such things, most game managers feel that crow predation is only the final stroke in a series of events that doomed eggs and ducklings from the start.

During his classic study of the blue-winged teal, Dr. Logan Bennett found "pecks of crow-destroyed [duck] eggs" around Iowa marshes—but noted that practically all of these had been promiscuously dropped before serious nesting had begun. They did not represent destroyed nests, nor eggs that would have hatched. He also found that heavy predation on ducklings was most likely to occur during drought periods when large numbers of young ducks were confined to shrinking water areas.

A ring-necked pheasant nest that is destroyed by crows is likely to be one that had problems from the beginning. For example, a nest that's barely hidden in a meager strip of fence-line grass between two open fields. Or a hayfield nest that is discovered in time by a farmer who mows around it and leaves it undamaged in a tiny island of unmown clover. To a passing crow, that little deviation from the norm is intensely interesting. And once he learns that such a place may hold pheasant eggs, he never forgets.

The furies of Hell are transcended not by woman scorned, but by Crow enraged.

A sample of that superfury was once loosed on my old friend

Bruce Stiles, late director of the Iowa Conservation Commission, when he was a young game officer stationed along the Missouri River in the early 1930s. Late one day during the waterfowl season he was walking alone across one of the Missouri's vast sandbars when he found a crippled crow. There were geese in the area and Bruce was reluctant to fire a shot, so he tried to dispatch the crow with a pole cut from a sandbar willow. However, the makeshift club proved too light and resilient to do the job. And as Bruce chased the fluttering bird across the open land, lashing at it with the limber pole, the crow set up a clamor of pain and alarm.

It was the time of day when far-foraging crows are beginning to converge on the great river roosts, and may loaf on the river's immense sandbars before flying to their roosts. Almost at once, angry crows arrived—materializing out of nowhere in the way crows will in such situations. The first shock troops quickly grew into a great mass of birds, their rage and frenzy intensified by the steady arrival of reinforcements. Within minutes, Bruce was the nucleus of a raging horde of crows. He never knew if there were hundreds or thousands; it was simply a roaring black cloud that engulfed him. He was being struck about the head and shoulders, and as he averted his face and shielded his eyes from attack, a striking bill laid open his unguarded cheek. Bruce was carrying a seven-shot 12-gauge gun, which was then lawful for waterfowling, and emptied the full magazine into the mass of birds. He loaded again, trying to protect head and face as he did so, and triggered another seven-shot volley. A 12-bore gun firing express loads at close range is a thunderous weapon, but the second volley had no more effect than the first—if anything, it only heightened his attackers' fury. Bruce beat a fighting retreat to the shelter of a distant willow thicket, and only then did the crows begin to draw away.

I can half-remember the old tales of hunters who spoke with respect and wonder of the mob frenzy of embattled crows, warning of the risks that a lone gunner might face. I always discounted such yarns, regarding them as rural precursors of Daphne du Maurier's "The Birds." But since then I have known

Bruce Stiles—and have often hunted crows over owl decoys.

For pure, unalloyed hatred, nothing in nature can compare to Crow's attitude toward the large owls. Housecats and hawks can incite crows, but their fullest fury is reserved for their living nightmare.

To Crow, a large owl is every dark and fearful dream come true. All of Crow's wit and wisdom is to no avail against the onslaught of Owl, and all crows know it. In the black mid-watches of the night, a great horned owl will sweep through a roost like the Angel of Death, soft and silent and consummately deadly. Nor is it just a matter of one owl seizing one crow; the owl may strike repeatedly, feasting only on heads and brains. It is a nightmare that Crow remembers through all the daytimes of his life, regarding owls with a primal dread and hatred that most men have happily forgotten.

When Crow discovers a great horned owl during the security of daylight, there is an instant clamor. From near and far, shrieking crows rally to the special battle cry that seems reserved for such times, crowding around the owl in a whirl of outrage. In full light they are more than a match for their enemy, and they press the advantage as Owl glowers at their insults, strangely reluctant to fight back. There is a running debate about whether crows actually strike an owl, but I have crept to within easy binocular range and watched crows strike feathers from the back of a wild, unrestrained great horned owl. (But never from the front, with those baleful eyes and terrible feet.) Crows could surely destroy an owl if they were willing to pay the price, but I've never heard of them doing so. Not a living owl, anyway.

When one of my classmates in graduate college was doing pheasant research in northern Iowa, he sometimes managed to work in a bit of crow hunting. Early one fall he borrowed a mounted snowy owl from his major professor's collection, attached the owl to a tall pole, and erected it in a woodlot on his study area. The results were something less than spectacular; during most of the morning he never fired a shot. Come noon, he left the decoy in place and joined his farmer-cooperator at lunch. Five cups of good Norwegian coffee later, Chris returned to his blind. A band of crows was just retiring with victorious jeers, the decoy had vanished, and the woodlot was white with a blizzard of owl feathers.

Winter coming on. Time for the Grand Reunion.

Some northern crows never do migrate, but the typical crow is as migratory as any other passerine bird and undertakes a journey that is as prompt and methodical as a robin's. It's not usually far. Few crows migrate more than five hundred miles— going just far enough to assure themselves of food supplies that won't be locked up by prolonged snow cover.

Most of the crows reared in the north tend to winter in our mid-latitudes between the 40th and 35th parallels. At the eastern end of this band there is a great center of wintering crow populations in the vicinity of Chesapeake Bay and its tributaries. One of the midwestern centers is near the junction of the Ohio and Mississippi rivers. A little farther west, large numbers of crows winter along the Arkansas and Missouri rivers. From early December to February, immense populations of crows concentrate in the regions that lie just south of winter and just north of spring. In 1886, ornithologist Samuel Rhoads said: "In winter a radial sweep of 100 miles, described from the city of Philadelphia and touching the cities of New York, Harrisburg, and Baltimore, will include in the daytime in its western semi-circle fully two-thirds of the crows inhabiting North America, and at night an equal proportion in its eastern half." Which wasn't true, of course. Similar claims could have been made all the way out to Kansas City, and beyond. The part to believe isn't Rhoads' flawed conclusion but the impression that inspired it, for the daily flights of crows to and from their great winter roosts might lead a man to say almost anything.

Such roosts may be small in area, but huge in terms of occupancy. In 1886 and 1887, up to 200,000 crows occupied twenty acres in Arlington National Cemetery. There was a twenty-five-acre grove in New Jersey near Hainesport that held as many as 300,000 birds. In Pennsylvania, the twenty-acre Davis Grove in Montgomery County had over 200,000 crows.

The immense winter roosts in the vicinity of Chesapeake Bay caught the attention of early naturalists, and both Wilson and Audubon wrote graphic accounts of some of the great crow roosts they had visited there.

The general localities of some roosts have been used for centuries, and individual roosts may extend beyond the memories of the oldest men. The main criterion, of course, is shelter. Roosts may be in thick conifers—not necessarily large trees, but dense enough to give good protection during storm periods. Or the roosts may be in deciduous groves, and on some islands in the Delaware River the roosts were in reeds, coarse patches of grass, and low brushwood. The big Arsenal Island roost in the Mississippi River at St. Louis provided trees for roosting in ordinary weather, and during severe weather and storm periods the crows often spent the night on the island's snow-covered sandbars or even on the ice shelves that surrounded it.

The greatest crow concentrations today are surely in prairie regions where gun pressure is light, human population is thin, and wintering conditions are ideal. There is a big catalpa grove in central Kansas today that is said to harbor ten million crows in midwinter. State Forestry, Fish, and Game Director Richard Wettersten found this hard to believe—until he saw it. "I don't know how many there are," Dick told me recently. "But when you get into a roost that size a few zeros more or less don't have much meaning. It's beyond comprehension, no matter how you figure it."

The biggest crow roost I've ever seen was on the north side of Lake Fort Cobb, about fifty miles southwest of Oklahoma City. For years, crows had wintered there on a south-facing slope that was densely grown with jack oaks, few of which were much over twenty feet high. Relatively safe (it was on state parklands), this roost was somewhat sheltered from northern wind and was in a region where peanuts and other crops were generally accessible all winter.

We never knew how many crows there were in that roost. It was commonly held that there were at least eight million birds during the roost's peak occupancy during January, but Karl

Jacobs, then game chief of the Oklahoma Department of Wildlife Conservation, flatly denied that. "It's a ridiculous exaggeration," Dutch used to say, "and I doubt if there have ever been more than four million crows in that roost!"

How many were there, really? Pick a figure. My conservative training used to limit me to a million, but you could quadruple that and no one would argue. I only know that when I first saw it, it was one of those crowd phenomena that rank with July in Disneyland.

We would stay at the Lakeside Motel just across the sandy road from the main roost, and sometimes when there was no moon I would sneak over into the roost to hear the universal mutter and babble that went on all night. From a short distance away it was like the sound of an ocean at flood tide, or night wind blowing through a forest of pliant trees—the ceaseless murmur of an indescribable multitude of large birds talking in their sleep. From closer in, it would resolve to low warbles that were strangely robinlike, or muted henlike cluckings and a wild assortment of grumblings and night-mewings, but rarely any *caw* fragments or anything that resembled conventional crow noises. The crow has seven pairs of syringeal muscles that give it a wide range of vocalization—and the subtle undertones of that range can be heard only in a crowded roost on a moonless winter night. It's been said that Satan never really sleeps. Nor do his imps, apparently.

With the approach of day, in the limbo of light and darkness that my Ozark friends say is "before the crow and after the owl," the muttering would begin to take on definition. The roost was awakening.

For about an hour the crows stayed put, shifting about and expressing themselves in a rising babble. It was as if they were staying in bed to organize their thoughts about the day's work, and in no particular hurry to be up and at it. If a few crows flew up out of the trees, the main host would shout angrily, telling them to get the hell back in bed and stop bucking for promotion. Finally, however, several thousand crows would take wing and begin milling above the main roost, yelling down at their com-

panions and making wild threats and promises. This would
ignite a wild enthusiasm that could be heard several miles away
on a quiet morning, and an immense canopy of crows would rise
out of the trees and begin streaming out to the day's feeding
points.

They dispersed widely, often thirty miles or more, hunting
that Main Chance. During the day their numbers were unim-
pressive, although we could always see a few crows feeding in
fields, and bits of black embroidery in the high Oklahoma sky.

But by late afternoon, the day's work nearly over, they would
begin staging in hedgerows, creek bottoms, and woodlots, gathering by tens and hundreds for the return home. Their great
numbers were again becoming apparent. This was not as obvious if there was a strong wind that kept the return flights close
to the ground. But on quiet days the crows would come streaming in high, the flocks coalescing into clouds, and the clouds
stretching in unbroken streams of black freebooters that sometimes spanned the horizons, growing ever denser as the dark
legions converged on the main roost. On such days when they
approached the roost area from on high, they might plunge
almost straight downward for a thousand feet, and then flash
falconlike with half-closed wings over treetops and fields. They
would rarely go directly to the roost during clear, quiet evenings,
but loafed in adjacent fields between sunset and bedtime, not
settling into the roost until full dark.

We've often wondered, watching a settling-in, if there is an
order of seniority. Crows roosting in lower parts of the trees are
often whitewashed by morning; can this be a sign of social
ordering? And are the dominant crows the whitewashers or the
whitewashees? As a whitewashee of some experience, I can't say
much for being on the receiving end. But I can't say much for
roosting in a treetop, either.

We were usually at Fort Cobb to hunt crows, which is not to say
that we hunted the roost. This is simply never done by bonafide
crow hunters who prefer to work miles from a roost with
mouth-blown call and camouflage, meeting crows on ground

where both hunter and bird must be at their best. Our gunning was done far out along the flyways during the day, and never in or near the main concentration

I can remember unproductive days when ten hours of effort earned us little more than the sand in our eyes and the growl in our bellies, and other days when we grew slug-nutty from gun recoil. But f␣r some reason, more than anything else, I recall the Dance on Monkey Mountain.

There is a singular mound rising out of the flat sandy country north of Fort Cobb. We never knew why it was called Monkey Mountain, nor did any of the locals, but it was obviously a checkpoint for the morning crow run.

A friend and I were lurking in the Mailbox Blind early one day, not far away. There was a bitter, gritty wind gusting out of the Panhandle, sweeping up the flanks of Monkey Mountain as a flight of late-rising crows arrived. They appeared over the distant mound dipping and rising, hanging above the summit with a wild display of aerobatics, bouncing and rolling in the wind currents and sometimes seeming to fly backward. This first bunch of hot pilots was joined by others until there were probably fifty crows up there, dancing in a stacked aerial ballet that must have lasted ten minutes. We'd never seen anything like it, and it puzzled us until my companion exclaimed: "Why, I'll be damned if they don't seem to be enjoying themselves!"

It must have been crazy up there, some erratic and violent combination of wind currents above the summit. Yet, we were sure that those crows were not inextricably locked in currents from which they couldn't escape. They were handling themselves with confidence and a great deal of inventive skill, master aerialists at play, wrestling with the wild wind out of sheer exuberance, like an airline captain doing aerobatics in a vintage biplane on his day off.

Inevitably, a great roost draws the attention of men embittered by the real or imagined wrongs done them by crows.

Most often, such attention is expressed with shotguns as landowners work over the big roosts in an effort to kill as many as possible and drive the rest away. If they make a steady job of it, they'll probably disperse the crows and break up the main roost into a number of smaller roosts. In terms of actual decimation, it has practically no effect.

During the 1920s and 1930s, however, an efficient method of crow-killing was devised in large roosts.

At 4 A.M. on March 9, 1938, a crow roost near Sharon, Wisconsin, was dynamited, killing "well over 5,000 crows." But this was admitted to be of "small account" when compared to the great bombings in more southerly roosts.

There was a time when Oklahoma roosts were regularly bombed in an effort, ill-advised or not, to control crop depredation. An Oklahoma crow bomb consisted of a crude sheet-iron tube about twelve inches long and three inches in diameter, with a wire hook at the open end. A stick of dynamite was inserted in this tube, and a couple of pounds of iron pellets poured in around the explosive. During the day, when the crows were gone, trees in the roost were festooned with bombs hung at all elevations; they were wired in series and detonated electrically.

The blast came late at night when the roost was filled with sleeping crows. Sometimes, as in the Wisconsin shot, the circuit was closed just before dawn—and perhaps on a Friday night or early Saturday morning so that schoolchildren would be available to gather dead crows. Through all the annals of man's relentless persecution of wildlife, nothing can compare to the instantaneous carnage that occurred when a roaring storm of shrapnel and a wave of concussion swept through a crowded crow roost. Near Harrisburg, Illinois, a thousand steel cannisters containing dynamite and scrap iron were hung in a roost and detonated at one time, and next morning 100,000 dead crows were picked up.

We haven't heard of a great roost-bombing for years, which isn't to say that roosts aren't still being destroyed.

Our friend Floyd Kringer, an Illinois game biologist, believes that his crow populations are thinner than they were a few years ago—and he knows why.

Back in 1951, Floyd and a friend checked the crow populations along the Kaskaskia River bottoms in southwestern Illinois. On one route they made twenty-one stops and had "canopies of birds" over them at nineteen of those stops. But that was when the Kaskaskia bottoms were prime country. For example, there was one farmer who controlled a solid square mile of big timber in the bottoms—a tangled maze of little backwater sloughs and oxbow ponds, with broad flats of alluvial timber with huge burr oaks and soft maples. Today, that entire 640 acres of wild floodplain timber is gone, replaced by corn and soybeans. Floyd has no doubt that the local crow decline wasn't caused by shooting (he doesn't know of a single dedicated crow hunter in his territory today) but by habitat losses that have destroyed prime roosting and nest sites. There are still crows along the Kaskaskia, and doubtless always will be, but not in the numbers that were met there before the stream channelizers began making the world safe for soybeans.

Are there fewer crows nationally than there were twenty years ago? Perhaps there are—although U.S. Fish and Wildlife Service reports don't tend to support this. The breeding bird survey that is conducted each June in the United States and parts of Canada indicates no significant change in the continental crow population from 1966 to 1974. There appeared to be a slight population upturn in the East and a slight downturn in the West during this period, but each balanced the other out. When a statistical regression is plotted for that eight-year period, the curve is flat—indicating no significant population change one way or the other.

If these surveys are valid, is our impression of fewer crows invalid? Not necessarily. The apparent decline of crows in some areas could reflect a fragmentation of crow concentrations as a result of roost destruction, and a widescale reduction in the sizes of crow flocks.

At any rate, recent federal regulations governing crow hunting don't actually reflect a decrease in the national crow population. When the U.S.-Mexico Migratory Bird Treaty was amended in 1972, Mexico insisted on specifically including *Corvidae* in an effort to protect certain jays. Crows were part of the package. As a result, federal law now limits crow hunting in the forty-eight contiguous states to a season not to exceed 124 days each year. The states are given an option to set season dates, limits, shooting hours, methods of take, or whatever—but crows may not be sport-hunted during peak nesting periods or taken by any means except firearms, archery, or falconry. However, none of this applies to crow control in cases of actual or impending depredation, or when crow concentrations may endanger public health. In an odd reversal of priorities, roost-bombing is not outlawed by the new regulations—which curtail the use of a shotgun and a dozen decoys but freely permit dynamite cannisters to be hung in the nesting groves and winter roosts of a protected migratory bird. It's all very confusing, but Crow will probably figure it out before we do.

It is likely, and appropriate, that a coyote will use the bones of the last man as a scent post. Beyond that, it's just as likely that the bones of the last coyote will be picked clean by Crow. If any critter was designed to endure and ultimately prevail, it is Crow. Brigand and buffoon, forever adjusting and adapting and cocking a suspicious eye at the situation, he'll hang in there from sheer perversity, his own bird to the last. As poet Ted Hughes wrote: "Crow—flying the black flag of himself." And at the end, when Crow follows the long procession of species out of a world grown cold under its dying sun, he'll exit laughing.

Day of the Crane

THE PLATTE IS A CRANE RIVER—a mile wide, an inch deep, and tall with birds. Flowing across Nebraska, it is a wild corridor of sandbars and shallows—a broad prairie stream designed by Providence for the wading and roosting of the lesser sandhill crane.

It is a different river than it was last fall. Snowmelt and ice jams have scoured and filled, the braided channels have shifted, and new shoals are building. It is a river of incessant change. But in all the changes there is one constant: the coming of the cranes.

They arrive in early March, up from such places as the Bitter Lakes of the Pecos in New Mexico and the Muleshoe Refuge of west Texas, some flying nonstop for 600 miles or more. It was spring when they left; by the time they reach the Platte they are overtaking winter. Here they wait, feeding and courting while spring catches up with them—hundreds of thousands of birds staging for the grand passage into northern Canada and Alaska.

Now it's a new day, the sun rising out of a prairie horizon so distant that the roosting cranes cast shadows 30 yards long

155

across the beaten-metal surface of the river. In an hour the March sky will teem with cranes going into the feeder fields, and the March morning will ring with their whinnying, trumpeting cries. They will be gone in early April, but their passage is memorable. They broke winter, and brought spring to the Platte again.

Only yesterday the Platte was a cold maze of dun sandbars and gray channels, empty of life. The riverside groves of cottonwoods and willows were bleak and skeletal, and there were no sounds but the crow and the wind and the whisper of water around the towheads in the channels.

Overnight it has been transformed, teeming with life and motion as the lesser sandhill cranes return to their special river. The lifeless sandbars suddenly wear gray forests of cranes, the vast flocks melting into the hazes upstream. There is a gusty beat of huge pinions, and a wild medley of clucks, courtship noises, flight calls and choruses, alarm signals, and the low constant mutter of myriad birds. Each night they will roost on the shoals and sandbars; early each morning they will head out into the feeder fields. Children riding in yellow buses to the consolidated schools will see fields filled with the great birds— the first and best lesson of the day, and one that a few wise teachers will build on.

There will be white-fronted geese coming any time now to this part of the Platte, with a scattering of blues and snows and a few early ducks. But center stage belongs to the sandhills. No other migrants can match their numbers, sounds, or performance. It is the day of the crane.

Specifications for lesser sandhill crane: plumage gray in adults, brownish in the youngsters. A fussy pompadour at one end; an iron stiletto at the other. In between: a chestnut forehead of bare skin, eyes like binoculars, and the voice of a whinnying Pegasus. Height 3½ feet, wingspan up to 6 feet, weight up to 8 pounds. Underpinning sufficient to reach ground from body, often through water. Appetite constant and considerable: seeds, berries, tubers, green salads, mice, lemmings, small snakes, waste grains, crustaceans, sand, and the odd pebble. Range: Mexico to

Siberia. Flight ceiling: between the thunder and the sun. Grazer, hunter, fisher. At home on uplands or in wetlands—a water bird gone afield. One of the old prairie breed, first cousin to the whooping crane, but far more durable and fortunate. A comedian touched with pathos and grandeur.

Egrets and herons fly with legs extended and necks curved back. Such neck-curved birds are graceful enough, but give an impression of Sunday aviators out for a turn around the field. Not so with the cranes. Flying cranes are like flung javelins, their necks and legs fully extended, reaching hungrily for distance. They are compass needles pointed north, spanning great gulfs of northern sky and taking their journeys seriously.

The fires of spring burn strangely in the lesser sandhill crane. A courting pair that meets on a feeding ground will greet each other with deep bows and high leaps into the air, interspersed with hops and two-steps, and again, the low courtly bows. Sometimes scores of the big birds will join in, looking like tipsy stilt-walkers trying to dance a minuet. It is deadpan comedy at its best—solemn and ungainly, with the timing just a bit off and the imminent chance of everyone getting all tangled up and taking a pratfall—but underlain with hope and affection, and something that is oddly beautiful.

There are more lesser sandhill cranes on the Platte River than there were twenty years ago. Once reason is the general prosperity of the birds themselves, and it may be that other migration stops have changed in some ways, or even vanished.

As a crane river, the Platte has suffered a number of man-made changes. Yet much of it flows as it always has, broad and shallow with wild buffer zones of cottonwoods and willows, and nearby croplands for gleaning and grazing. And while the Platte endures in much of its original form, and so long as there are migrations of cranes, the two will get together.

But for 30 years a certain project has simmered on the bureaucratic back burner. If it ever comes to full boil, some of the best parts of this crane river will vanish.

The Midstate Reclamation Project was first proposed in the early 1940s, subsequently embraced by the Bureau of Reclamation, and officially authorized in 1967. Under this scheme, a system of dams, reservoirs, and canals would be built to foster irrigation projects. The Platte would be dammed, and its waters diverted into holding reservoirs. Long stretches of the river would be dried up for most of the year. As such channels are choked with vegetation, reducing their capacity to handle flood flows, they would be prime targets for channelization—to the ultimate ruin of the channels and miles of riparian forests. Ironically, many Nebraska farmers oppose the diversion idea, claiming that it is a wasteful boondoggle that they do not need. But such minor details are not likely to deter promoters who have caught the heady scent of federal funds.

In terms of wildlife, it could be a crushing blow. There is more to the central Platte than the clouds of sandhill cranes against a March sunset. As a wild corridor through intensely cultivated landscapes, the river draws whooping cranes, bald eagles, deer, beaver, waterfowl, shorebirds, and hosts of lesser wildlife. Some supporters of Midstate shrug off such losses by suggesting that the wildlife simply go elsewhere. They would be well-advised to follow their own suggestion; we can even tell them where to go.

But for now, it is enough to know that the river still runs free, still braiding its old way across the prairies. The cranes are back, and so is spring.

North Again

EARLY MARCH ON THE CANADIAN PRAIRIES is just another name for winter.

Oh, there's been some loose talk about spring coming, but not much to back it up. Cabin fever is rising. Vast numbers of small boys are getting whacked. Folks are edgy, and neighbors coming home from Mexican holidays are well advised to lie low and keep quiet until their suntans fade.

But now, for our old friends in Saskatoon, Moose Jaw, and Portage la Prairie, we're happy to verify that rumor of spring. Due south of you, the Cheyenne Bottoms of central Kansas are newly alive with ducks and geese. They're bringing spring up from the Gulf Coast and will be with you directly. Hang in there. The Grand Passage is under way. Spring is being delivered by our most dependable airline.

An excited, restless throng is coming up through the heart of North America—up from the wintering marshes and estuaries, from the Sabine and Aransas and Laguna Madre. Their impatience builds with each passing day, the hosts of wildfowl crowding behind the frost barrier of the 32-degree isotherm and pushing it steadily northward.

Most of them are being drawn to a vast arc of open land that sprawls through southeastern Alberta, southern Saskatchewan, and southwestern Manitoba, down into those parts of the Dakotas and Montana that lie east and north of the Missouri River. This is the prairie pothole region—the fabled Duck Factory—300,000 square miles of the richest duck-producing range in the New World.

It's a young landscape, no older than the retreat of the last lobes of the Wisconsin glaciation perhaps 10,000 years ago. Sheets, ridges, hills, and mounds of ground-up, heaved-up glacial junk were strewn over thousands of square miles—a rumpled landscape with a remarkable faculty for retaining surface waters. Lakes and ponds were dammed by countless glacial moraines; others were trapped in the oxbows of Pleistocene rivers. Some resulted from ice lenses—the soil-covered chunks of ice left buried in the debris after the glacial retreat, later melting to leave water-filled depressions. It is a baby land, raw and new, still too young to have developed mature drainage systems. That will come, of course, when stream courses and river valleys deepen. The lakes and ponds not drained will eventually fill, choke, and die.

But that is long away, and now, in a wet year, the region may have eight million potholes, sloughs, lakes, and marshes that are enormously productive of waterfowl. Thousands of square miles of this region average an incredible density of over thirty-one breeding ducks per square mile—and although the prairie pothole region is only ten percent of the continent's total waterfowl breeding area, it produces at least half of the continent's ducks.

It's more than just abundance of water. The glacial tills, clays, and rock scourings that form the bed of this region are immensely rich in minerals. The young soils born of these parent materials have not been subjected to heavy precipitation nor efficient drainage, and the mineral wealth has not been leached out of the upper levels of soil. Much of it remains within reach of plant roots, to be recycled into standing plant parts. Water flowing over and through these prairie soils conveys a rich charge of nutrients to the prairie pond. The slightly alkaline water and warm summers of the prairie region promote rapid decomposition of plant materials in both soil and water, and filling of the ponds with plant debris is retarded. Even the occasional drought benefits these waters, for the organic stuff in their basins will break down even faster if aired and sunned.

The subhumid prairie climate not only built a deep grassland humus rich in nitrogen and phosphorus, charging the glacial wetlands with fertility, but made a prairie biome that is far more attractive to waterfowl than is forest.

The myriad potholes, ponds, and marshes of the northern prairie region offer waterfowl an incredible number of varied, interspersed habitats. No two potholes or marshes are alike. Their basic fertility provides lush vegetation and high production of plankton and insect life. They offer wildfowl escape cover, nesting cover, brood cover, loafing sites, and food in an abundance and variety that are incomparable, and between these richly varied waters there are fields and grasslands for feeding and nesting. Now, in early spring, this life-kettle is beginning to simmer.

They began pulling out of some wintering grounds in January, staging northward for as long as two and a half months with an urgency that grows with the strengthening sunlight. The vanguard of the waterfowl migration may reach the prairie potholes of southern Canada as early as mid-March, when Arctic owls are still adorning fenceposts like caps of snow and flocks of snow buntings whirl across the bleak fields. Any gains made during the day are lost at night, when newly thawed waters refreeze. Beneath a veneer of cold mud the ground is still frozen, and bitter winds sweep the openlands. But the ducks are not misled; they believe the zenith of the sun.

Mallards and pintails and Canada geese are the first to come, followed by gadwalls, shovellers, baldpates, teal, and scaup. Although the big marshes and lakes are closed with rotting ice, sheet water covers old wheat stubble fields and a few marsh edges are beginning to open. There may be no green foods for a month after the first migrants arrive, nor any new cover for nesting. The vanguards are content to eat seeds and nest in last year's dry vegetation.

Many of the prairie ducks begin pairing long before they reach the northern marshes. Prenuptial courtship was under way on the wintering grounds as early as January; most of the mallards are now paired, and many of the pintails. For these, the intense competition of prenuptial courting is almost over—most of the ducks have accepted their drakes, pair bonds have formed, and the mated birds fly low over the warming April marshes and ponds. Blue and snow geese have arrived at the prairie region, tarried briefly, and pressed northward to their nesting grounds. (And how can we forgive the taxonomists for discarding the old name of the snow goose, *Chen hyperborea*, "the goose from beyond the north wind?") The whistling swans have come and gone, keeping their tryst with the subarctic. Some Canada geese may nest in the prairie regions, but most of them, too, are drawn farther north. The prairie pothole country is left to the myriad ducks.

In spring mornings and evenings there are ducks everywhere in the prairie skies. Gadwalls are beginning to spark in earnest. So are the baldpates, those tardy lovers, among the last of the dabbling ducks to pair off. Canvasbacks perform their most breathtaking aerial rite—the drake closely pursuing the duck and seizing her tail with his bill in a game of crack-the-whip at nearly sixty miles per hour and only twenty feet above the yellowed marsh tules.

High over the prairie an echelon of pintails is in prenuptial courtship with several drakes pursuing an unmated duck. These bull sprigs are at their showiest and best—agile, swift, and ardent—but the duck gracefully outmaneuvers them. A high-speed ballet far above the greening prairies in the long April twilight, with the land in shadow below and courting wildfowl still in the sun above. The hen pintail glows like old gold in the late sun, and as the drakes wheel swiftly into the light their white neckstocks and upper breasts are suffused with salmon.

At last the ducks have made their choices. Unmated males go puttering off into idleness and bachelorhood. Mated pairs keep to themselves. Now the evening flights are searchflights, the paired birds examining the prairie waters and fields for nesting sites that fill their requirements.

For diving ducks such as redheads, canvasbacks, and ruddy ducks, such a site is emergent vegetation growing in water. In a band of cattails or hardstem bulrush a few yards from open water, the duck begins weaving stems into a strong, well-made basket platform that may rise a foot or more above the surface of the water—often complete with approach ramp leading up to the nest. The drake doesn't help. Not that the duck really needs him. Given good materials, she works fast and builds well. There may be times, during heavy spring rains, when a hen canvasback may race with rising floodwaters in an effort to raise her nest. In only a few hours she can raise her nest several inches, skillfully building beneath a clutch of eggs.

The puddle ducks—mallards, pintails, teal, and other dabblers—seek nesting sites on dry ground. This can be a haystack, in a field or meadow hundreds of yards from water, or in a patch of sedge only a few feet from the pond.

There the duck makes her "scrape"—the shallow nesting bowl in the earth that is unlined when she begins her clutch of eggs. She finishes the nest as her egg-laying proceeds, adding plant-stuffs that are within reach while she's on the nest and pulling over any high grasses to form a canopy. She plucks feathers from her breast and belly, and the completed clutch of eggs will lie on a nest lining of dried grasses and starbursts of down—a mattress of great warmth and softness.

During the laying period the drakes still attend their mates, joining the ducks when they are not on the nest and flying and feeding with them. Some species, such as blue-winged teal, tend to stay together far into incubation time. But mallards and pintails leave their hens soon after laying is completed and incubation has begun. The drakes resort to loafing spots, joining the bachelors. They've been declared surplus, with nothing more exciting to do than sit around on muskrat houses and watch each other's feathers drop out in the summer molt.

Of all northern prairie marshes, the Delta Marsh is the most famous.

Lying at the south end of Lake Manitoba about sixty miles from Winnipeg, it is one of the great continental magnets for waterfowl, which in turn draws hunters, scientists, naturalists, artists, writers, and photographers. This is the setting for H. Albert Hochbaum's classic *The Canvasback on a Prairie Marsh* and *Travels and Traditions of Waterfowl*, and Lyle Sowls' *Prairie Ducks*. Delta has had a lot of good press, and deservedly.

I've never been sure whether Delta lies at the south end of Lake Manitoba or whether it *is* the south end of Lake Manitoba. For two thousand years, spring winds have driven ice packs onto shoals at the end of the vast, shallow lake, the grinding slabs overriding themselves and plowing into the lake bottom to bulldoze sand up into a long, narrow ridge. North of this natural levee is open lake. South of it is the great marsh itself—about 36,000 acres of plume-topped phragmites cane, bulrush, cattails, broad ponds and bays, and little secret potholes.

The marsh is connected to Lake Manitoba by several passes cut through the lake ridge, and its great open bays fluctuate with the lake levels and prevailing wind. Here are some of the most extensive stands of phragmites in the world—their ten-foot stems forming incredibly dense jungles that are analogs of African papyrus swamps. Through these jungles of huge grasses are waterways that may choke out and vanish, or open into great shining bays of clear water. The creeks and bays are essentially parts of the main lake itself, connected to it by the passes that break the lake ridge. Lying within the phragmites stands are isolated sloughs and little ponds that are born of snowmelt and rainfall and have no ties with the lake. These shallow, hidden waters are a wealth of submerged aquatic plants—sago pondweed, coontail, horned pondweed, and many more, with belts of cattails and bulrush that stand against the walls of phragmites. Sometimes, in high water, it is possible to drive a canoe back into some of these isolated sloughs. But during low water, when there are no routes through the depths of the phragmites, the only access is from the sky.

That wooded lake ridge abounds with birds. Thickly grown with ash, poplar, box elder, and some bur oak, the natural levee is never much more than a few hundred yards wide but stretches east and west for miles. In May it seems to be a stopover for about every songbird that is on its way to somewhere else, and many stay for nesting. I've never seen so many nesting northern orioles and yellow warblers; if there's another place with such oriole densities, I've not heard of it. Catbirds and warbling vireos abound in these lake-ridge thickets, and mourning doves—which were rare visitors in the 1930s—are nesting everywhere. Many of the transient passerines that kept going in May begin returning in July, their nesting completed, and the place teems with midsummer tree swallows.

In and around the lake-ridge thickets and out into the marsh are countless yellow-headed blackbirds and red-winged blackbirds. At the edges of the wet meadows are short-billed marsh wrens, and farther out in the hardstem bulrush and cattail edges are nests of long-billed marsh wrens. On islands of tules are noisy colonies of Franklin's gulls and Forster's terns, western grebes, and crowds of little eared grebes. Ease your canoe around a wall of phragmites and come upon one of these places unannounced. The marsh world tears itself into feathered fragments, with appropriate sound effects. Ears ringing, you retreat to a quiet, restful corner, only to run into a loose colony of black terns. If there's anything that can liven up a quiet moment on the marsh, it's nesting black terns. Cheeky little hellions. They've knocked my cap into the water and then combed my hair as I reached for it.

There are black-crowned night herons, American bitterns, pied-billed grebes, white pelicans, sora rails, and coots everywhere. And in the heart of the marsh—in the edges of sloughs and hardstem bulrush at the fringes of the great bays—are the divers: ruddy ducks, redheads, and the lordly canvasback. In a setting four miles wide and twenty miles long, there are more bays and channels and lost ponds than a strong paddler could explore in a summer, all set in a vast matrix of phragmites and tules. Al Hochbaum once said of it: "On calm, quiet mornings in May the prairie marsh floats lightly in a world of sky." It does indeed, and one's spirit floats with it. But in lowering weather the gray reaches of marshland can weigh heavy. Strange, how the alchemy of open sunlight can transform a leaden marsh and lift and lighten the spirit.

For scientists, Delta is an infinitely complex organism whose value grows as the supply of such organisms dwindles. This is the site of the famous Delta Waterfowl Research Station and the nearby University of Manitoba Field Station. Delta is mainly concerned with waterfowl ecology and management; the Manitoba station deals with broader marsh ecology. Both are training grounds; at Delta alone there have been over a hundred master's and doctoral degrees earned by graduate students from dozens of colleges and universities. It is a superbly organized field station with laboratories, living quarters, and an excellent library. The director of the Delta station today is Peter Ward—biologist, artist, advisor, and a marsh hand of vast personal mileage. No man knows Delta better than Pete Ward—unless it's Al Hochbaum himself. Al is retired director of the Delta station and one of North America's premier waterfowl authorities. He still lives at the station—his forty-year love affair with the Delta as ardent as ever.

Fifty miles west of Delta and the broad flats of the Portage Plains, the land begins to lift and fold. It rises into a plateau 1,500 feet above sea level—a lovely farmscape with clumps and groves of pale-barked aspen, neat farmsteads, and fields of cereal grains. And everywhere, jewel-like little potholes fringed with dark bulrush, the brighter greens of cattails, and the creamy green of whitetop grass. This is the famed Minnedosa pothole region, a rare meld of highly productive grainlands and equally productive ducklands.

One evening just at sundown we took a short flight over this country. To the east, the plateau fell away to the flatlands of Lake Manitoba. To the north it continued to rise, darkening and roughening into the bush of the huge Riding Mountain National

Park. As far to the south and west as we could see from 3,000 feet, the country was a fortune in silver coins strewn over a rumpled green cover. Potholes, ponds, marshes and marshlets, lakes and lakelets by the thousand, by the tens of thousands. The shape and character of these little pockets of water are infinitely varied. Some are quite round, others are ovoid, angular, crescent-shaped, elongated. Some are hundreds of acres. Others can be measured in square yards. They are everywhere; the traveler is never out of sight of them. Just south of the town of Minnedosa is a hundred-square-mile study area being surveyed by a team of U.S. Fish and Wildlife Service biologists. The area has an average of eighty potholes per square mile, and there are square-mile sections that hold up to 140 potholes averaging one and a half acres in size.

The U.S. Fish and Wildlife team is studying canvasbacks in cooperation with the Canadian Wildlife Service. What is a good canvasback pond? What is its hydrology? What waterfowl foods does it produce, and how are the canvasbacks reproducing by age structure?

Which means censusing nesting canvasbacks in the potholes, a chore that consists of wading the edges and combing nesting cover without filling hip boots in the process—efforts that are wholly incompatible. It's a sweaty, leg-wearying business, wading thigh-deep through dense flooded vegetation, but never boring. Aside from the main feature of finding canvasback nests, there are endless short subjects. If I missed any of these, as I often did, biologist Jerry Serie would point them out to me. Jerry is a fieldman's fieldman, and a good one to prowl that country with.

In a biome simply boiling with life, there is always something to catch attention. While a nesting coot is having a hysterical collapse only a few yards away, a couple of black terns make a strafing run. There goes my cap again. And just beside the floating cap is a floating wad of bulrush stems and algae, its half-covered cavity filled with the tiny eggs of a horned grebe. A little farther, as we wade knee-deep through a dense stand of flooded whitetop grass, a hen mallard flushes beside me. Her nest is built over water, strong and substantial. It is well hidden, for whitetop stands are dense. Jerry submerges one of the eggs and judges it to be about eleven days into incubation. This is the first time I have ever seen a mallard nest built over water—which surprises Jerry far more than the nest itself, for it is a rather common thing in this country.

Mallards here in the Minnedosa potholes often build over water—a sharp departure from their usual tradition of nesting on dry land. Ron Gatti, a Wisconsin graduate student over in the East Meadows marshes on the other side of Lake Manitoba, tells me that as many as half of his mallards build nests over water. Such mallards are more likely to build over-water nests in bulrushes or cattails than in whitetop, but in any case it's a matter of emergency pioneering. On many of these waters, fields come almost to the edge, and a skimpy fringe of shoreline grass or sedge is heavily worked by predators. The mallards that build there often build out over water, à la canvasback. Ron doesn't think that they're as good at it as canvasbacks, but what the heck—I've never been much impressed by the few canvasback nests that I've seen built on dry land.

A little farther on, we check a canvasback nest that has been under surveillance for days. Big things happening. Yesterday there were nine eggs in the nest; now there are three. The others are newly hatched. One of the three remaining eggs is being pipped, and we can see draggled down feathers through an enlarging hole as the cap of the egg is cut away. The canvasback duck is close by with her other babies, and we get out of there.

The Minnedosa potholes seem hard-bottomed enough, lacking the soft flocculent muck that is known by such sobriquets as "loon puke" and other vivid terms you'll never find in the *Journal of Wildlife Management*. Yet, as we wade in the pothole edges and stir up bottom debris with our booted feet, there's that old familiar smell of marsh grass.

Our friend Paul Errington—who devoted his life to marshes and marsh doings—once took the urbane president of a great university to one of his research areas. Later, when asked what he thought of Paul's wild wetlands, the great man grimaced and

said: "It stinks." Which it did, of course, and still does and
always will. But it's all in the nose of the beholder. It tingles my
sinuses like the devilish fumes of a Yellowstone geyser basin, or
the pungent reek of skunk borne on fall wind and diluted with
distance, and maybe laced with campsmoke. And I know that
the smells themselves aren't the important thing—it's the images
they evoke. If I were a college president with no marsh memories, and no ken of wild wetlands and the vitality of these
magnificent support systems, then I suppose they'd only stink
for me, too.

The Delta Marsh is rich duck country. It produces many
wildfowl—although its greater value may be as an arrival point
for spring migrations, a summering area for bachelor puddle
ducks, and as a staging area for the great fall flights. In terms of
sheer production, however, it cannot match the Minnedosa.

There is an axiom of wildlife biology that the productivity of
a wildlife habitat is largely contingent on the interspersion of
types. Variety is the spice of life—and the Minnedosa potholes
are infinitely varied. No two are the same in size, depth, vegeta-
tive composition, shorelines, or uplands. Some are almost entirely open water; others are nearly filled with floating and emergent aquatics. One shoreline is thickly grown; another is open,
with prime loafing sites. Some potholes may offer sago pondweed tubers or smartweed seeds, or be richer in insect life than
others, or have better escape cover for duck broods. Variety is
enhanced by accessibility; no Minnedosa pothole is very far
from another. Which counts for a lot, since a duck and her brood
won't stay in a particular pothole if there's another within easy
walking distance. Ducks ramble a lot, moving from one water
area to another and relishing the change of scene. Ducks and
their flightless broods may travel up to a mile from the original
nest site. Pintail families are the most mobile; they rarely stay in
a single pothole for more than two weeks. No mallard brood has
been known to stay in one pothole for more than three weeks.
Ruddy ducks are the least mobile of all—which isn't surprising,
if you've ever seen a ruddy duck walk.

What with one thing and another, this is duck country supreme. The Minnedosa, in a good water year, may hold over a hundred breeding ducks per square mile and contribute at least a million ducks to the autumn flyways.

In a warm, light rain, my wife Dycie and I spent most of the June day out on the Delta Marsh, prowling down watery corridors between walls of phragmites and letting the breeze carry our canoe across the bays. There wasn't a whole lot going on. The gentlemen diving ducks had pulled out for their bachelor lakes, and the gentlemen puddle ducks still in residence were sulking because the lady puddle ducks wouldn't play—said ladies being off somewhere "with a loaf in the oven," as grandad used to say.

At about four o'clock we decided to hang it up. The rain had stopped, and the little breeze had died. We stripped off our rainshirts and rolled up our sleeves in the muggy air, and so we arrived at the last bay and headed up the narrow ditch to where the car was parked. There had been no insects out on the marsh, but when we entered that ditch, we entered banks of Delta mosquitoes.

In our ramblings around, we've known mosquitoes. On Mahogany Hammock in the Florida Everglades we once saw a skeeter so big that two wood ticks and a horseleech were attached to it. Another time, in the White River Bottoms in Arkansas, we were in clouds of mosquitoes so thick that you could reach out and grab and there'd be a sort of white place left hanging in the air. No josh.

But all that wasn't a patch on this narrow shoreline ditch in the Delta Marsh. We were using a Canadian repellent that's about as hot as any you can buy (95 percent N, N-diethyl-m-toluamide, the kind of stuff that can digest a watch crystal), and it was barely good enough. We made the landing in a gray, singing veil of insects, and set a new record for stowing gear and racking a canoe.

That evening Pete Ward stopped by our cabin. I sagely observed that it was a great night for bugs, and Pete replied seriously: "You know, most people regard this as tame country—safe and civilized. But out there tonight on the marsh edges, it's an incredibly hostile environment. I wonder if a lightly clad man could survive the night on one of those phragmites landings."

Which, in turn, caused me to wonder about the effects of this hostility on the creatures that are out there on such nights. Mosquitoes are active and voracious predators, and their collective effect is immense. They might not harm fully feathered birds, but what of newly hatched ducklings?

Waterfowl suffer heavy losses between hatching and feathering—a high-risk period when they are highly vulnerable to predation and all the sundry natural shocks that their tender flesh is heir to. Are mosquitoes an important cause of loss during this period? No one knows, although ducks have certainly coexisted with skeeters for a long time. They have, indeed, coexisted with a wide spectrum of predators and have adjusted well to a talon-and-fang world.

On the nesting prairies the three grades of waterfowl mortality are loss of eggs, loss of ducklings, and loss of adult ducks—in descending order of occurrence.

Crows are probably the most notorious egg predators. Originally uncommon in the northern prairies, they pioneered the pothole region with the first farmers and added a new dimension to the lives of northern waterfowl.

In his work at Delta, Lyle Sowls found that only 35 percent of 206 duck nests hatched successfully—and crows had destroyed 21 percent of the total. There were two types of crows involved. There were those nesting in trees near meadows where ducks nested, and whose predation on duck nests was usually in the immediate area. There were also crows wandering across the marshes for great distances, often in bands of a half-dozen birds or more. Such hunting crows are unmistakable; they fly with beaks pointed downward, heads twisting slightly, keen eyes searching. They are persistent and thorough—beating slowly into the wind and achieving maximum lift at a low speed, crossing marshes and meadows on efficient transects. Once across a marsh, they allow the wind to sweep them back to the far side again, and they begin crossing the marsh on a new course.

Hell hath no fury like that of a duck hunter being ripped off by Crow. Through the 1920s and 1930s, books and articles roundly condemned the black banditti, crying havoc and calling the brotherhood to arms. Elaborate campaigns were mounted. The Alberta game department set up a prize system in which hunting and fishing clubs competed for the largest numbers of crows and magpies killed. For a four-year period in the mid-1920s, there were from 45,000 to 107,000 crow eggs turned in annually in Alberta—and the adult crows and magpies tallied ranged from 22,000 to 45,000. Great works had been wrought. Or had they?

Alas, crows do not breed until the second spring after hatching, and unoccupied juvenile crows are likely to be among the most persistent duck predators. If the nests, eggs, and young of nesting adult crows are destroyed, these out-of-work birds may join the bands of juvenile egg-eaters that are out there working the marshes and meadows.

It is possible, too, that man may not only augment the number of crows hunting the marshes, but may unwittingly serve as bird dogs. Consider the eminent ornithologist who said: "The crow is the duck's worst enemy. I make this statement unreservedly . . . Exactly one week after I counted forty-two mallard nests, I found the crows had destroyed all but two of them."

I've little doubt that the good doctor had helped those crows. I know that I have, a few times. Crows watch lone men in marshes and shrewdly mark any effects of their presence—such as ducks flushed from nests. Much the same thing is true of certain mammals. I was once followed by a large striped skunk for a half-mile through low meadow and marsh edge. Tagging along thirty feet behind me, he seemed a healthy, normal animal, and my charm probably lay in the fact that I happened to be going in the direction that he wanted to go, and that I was breaking trail for him.

Skunks and Franklin ground squirrels both follow human trails through a marsh and will exploit any duck nests to which those trails are likely to lead. This is especially true in summer when grasses are green and lush and a man's trail is easily followed as he moves from nest to nest. As the nesting season wears on, and the marsh grows drier, skunks and ground squirrels tend to widen their cruising range as water barriers diminish. Not that a skunk needs dry ground for his work; Lyle Sowls and Pete Ward once found a skunk resting on a grassy couch ten inches high and two feet square in a wet meadow. Sudden encounters with skunks, by the way, are occupational hazards of marsh biology.

Until about forty years ago, the raccoon was almost nonexistent in the Delta and Minnedosa region. Since then it has come back from wherever it had gone (raccoons were there in the early times), and it has come back hungry. Raccoons are now abundant in some of the northern prairies that have been beyond the recent range of this species. Raccoons are rarely, if ever, mentioned in anything written about Delta or Minnedosa before 1945.

Today the raccoon may be the most serious of the nest predators—especially on canvasbacks and redheads. A water barrier that might deter most predatory mammals poses no problem for raccoons. A coon is fond of foraging around the edges of water, is an excellent swimmer, and relishes eggs. And after making a good meal of canvasback eggs, the rascal may curl up in the duck's nest and take a nap.

How serious is such predation? Again, no one is sure. There have been recent declines in the success of over-water nesters that might be attributed to a concurrent rise in raccoons. But with northern raccoon hides bringing $25 and more, the problem has a built-in solution.

If her nest is lost early in the season before incubation is well begun, there is a good chance that the duck will try again. Her renesting is a buffer against the special hazards of early spring, and she can often adjust to the raccoon that devours her eggs. She can never adjust to men who devour her marsh.

Lawrence King is a lean, weathered Manitoban who manages

the East Meadows Ranch east of Delta. It includes thousands of acres of rich marshland, and King's job is to keep it that way. He is a professional marsh manager, and he is angry and worried.

"In this interlake country between Lake Manitoba and Lake Winnipeg," he told us, "they're tearing out aspen and draining potholes as fast as they can. The land is going into oats, barley, alfalfa. As far north as The Pas, they are draining, draining! Even up there, some people would like to see all the Ducks Unlimited levees and water control structures destroyed, the wetlands drained, new pastures made. Anyplace where grass can conceivably grow, they want to put in cattle. No thought of tomorrow. They just want to add to the glut!"

Pete Ward is also concerned. He fears for duck production on the Portage Plains south of Delta, and its effect on Delta itself, and talks grimly about the pernicious draining and filling of the little Minnedosa potholes. And although many American wildlifers don't share such pessimism, the disturbing fact remains that King and Ward have lifetimes of perspective, while the Yanks come from torn, drained regions that are likely to make even dying Canadian wetlands look pretty good.

And are the northern prairies' potholes and marshlands really doomed?

Well, it's a cinch that we won't get many new ones until the next interglacial period, and it's doubtful that astrophysical forces can move faster than a government drainage agency that smells pork barrel.

As a geologic agent, of course, man isn't always the omnipotent hotshot he thinks he is. It's true that his works can greatly accelerate the siltation of natural basins and prematurely drain wetlands long before maturing natural drainage would have done the job right, creating quality natural rivers in the process. But premature drainage is unlikely to be permanent unless carefully maintained. Drain tiles break and clog, ditches cave in and fill, and with just a little lucky neglect a natural marsh may reassert itself. The tragedy is not that we destroy a marsh for all time, which we may not do, but in the fact that we destroy it for our time. We do not deny the ages the wonders of a wild marshland; we deny only ourselves and our children.

But those are winter thoughts, the sort that have put this frost in my hair. Time to think spring.

Years ago, after an extended field trip to the marshes of the Gulf Coast, Paul Errington reflected: "The South was genuine, beautiful, and fascinating, but it was not home to one born and apprenticed in a country molded by ice sheets."

He spoke for all children of the northern prairies and glacial wetlands—people and wildfowl. Even though the prairie ducks have basked this winter in the Laguna Madre and other sunny resorts, it has been in forced exile. They were banished from their homeland by winter and are chafing to return. The North is where they belong, and for seven months, from ice to ice, they will be back in their prairie waters. The seven months are beginning; the fires of spring are kindled.

North again. Home again.

Part IV

THE HORIZONS OF HOME

... and this prayer I make,
Knowing that Nature never did betray
The heart that loved her.
                    William Wordsworth

A Letter
to a Young Trapper

DEAR JOHNNY:

It was mighty good to see you last Saturday, and I was pleased to hear your mom say that you were planning to go into wildlife work. Wonderful! But remember how your dad and I laughed at the way we were dressed? He was wearing a new suit and I had on an old canvas Filson coat and faded jeans. Well, that's one difference between a successful newspaperman and a seedy wildlifer!

If your compass needle really is swinging toward a career in wildlife biology, let me sound off a bit. The two most important moves in your life are marrying the right girl and marrying the right job. Well, marrying the right girl is like good wingshooting—it's wonderful to do, but impossible to explain. So let's talk about the second point; it's a lot simpler.

In any line of work, you get what you pay for. Nothing worth having ever "jest comes"—it's gotta be fetched. In terms of the wildlife profession, that means all the schooling that you can get, and some pretty tough schooling it is, too.

Just because you like to hunt, fish, and trap doesn't mean that you're cut out for wildlife work, although it's a good tipoff. That's what drew most of us into it. For the life of me, I can't savvy why a man would *want* to be in wildlife work if he doesn't like to prowl around in the boondocks. Besides, real outdoor experience and the thousand skills that go with it is a basic requirement for a successful wildlife career. Your dad is a fine outdoorsman and can teach you a lot, so listen to Big John—he's your first real prof and the outdoors is your first classroom.

But just liking to hunt and fish aren't enough. You must want to dig deeper and be willing to study hard, and have a burning curiosity about what makes wild critters tick. That means field work. Days, months, years, a lifetime of intense field work, in all seasons, in all weather. And before, during and after that field work, you must never stop studying.

You're in high school now, and you'll need all the math, chemistry and biology you can get. Hit 'em hard, but at the same time don't neglect that English. Two of the greatest writers of our century were game and fish biologists: Aldo Leopold and Rachel Carson. The richest rewards in wildlife work today are for the men and women who are trained field biologists with a lot of outdoor mileage, and who know how to tell the story.

From here on, go after grades. Those C's won't do you much good. If you're really serious about a wildlife career, you'll want high school report cards loaded with A's and B's. You're not sure you're smart enough? Well, I think you are. Being smart is probably more a matter of guts and persistence than it is just brains—and I think you've got all three.

One of the surest losers I can think of is the high school swinger with a C average who decides to drift into wildlife biology because he likes to hunt and fish, and because it sounds easier than anything else. Well, even if he does get into college, he'll be clobbered by the competition he meets there. Today's wildlife majors are the smartest, hardest-working kids I've ever known, and they set a fast pace.

Wildlife schooling is no cinch. Your undergrad work in college will be loaded with organic and inorganic chemistry, physics, math ranging from algebra through calculus, geology, toxicology, histology, bacteriology, parisitology, embryology, statistics, scientific Russian or German, and many other courses. You'll be deep into your college career before you begin getting what you really came for: wildlife and fisheries management. And even then, it's not all khaki and field boots. You'll be taking limnology, mammology, and taxonomy—in which you may have to memorize the scientific classification of every fish and wildlife species in North America.

I hope I'm not scaring you. But remember, there ain't no Santa Claus.

A budding biologist shouldn't stop at the bachelor of science degree. He should go on for at least a master of science degree. The M.S. degree is now the minimum for a wildlife biologist, and many conservation agencies won't hire you without one. You don't go after advanced degrees just because they look cool after your name; it's in graduate school that you really begin to work on your own and do the independent field research that will be your lifetime job.

In other words, you'll be putting in at least five years of college, and maybe as many as eight, getting your training. But at the same time, don't neglect your education. They're two different things. Training is what you get in the classroom and lab; education is what you get out there in the woods, fields and marshes. Neglect neither. It's all very well, wearing a white lab coat and analyzing data within wide "limits of confidence." But somebody's got to get those data—and the quality of your research can be no better than the quality of your raw information. And *that* demands a guy with trained eyes and great stamina, a sharp observer who can also throw a diamond hitch over a mule pack or pole a canoe upstream in fast water. A scientist with callouses on his hands and the stain of weather on his face.

There'll be times during your career when all your hard work and training are thrown back in your face, and it hurts. You'll be a "college boy wildlife expert" to many people who still believe that a whiskery old guide back in the brush, with his gurgling pipe and mighty pronouncements about the outdoors, is the only man who knows anything about wildlife. But I'll never forget the night when such a guy challenged one of our veteran biologists at a public meeting, and said:

"Now you listen to me, college boy, and listen good! I've had thirty years of experience in the woods, and . . . "

Pete cut him down with: "Oh, no you haven't! I know you. You've had one year of experience thirty times, and there's a difference!" There sure is.

Some of the toughest, most seasoned outdoorsmen I've ever met have been wildlife biologists. They'll hold their own in any company, with horse, gun, axe or paddle, and they're mighty good guys to share a campfire with. But at the same time, so are countless outdoorsmen who have never seen the inside of a college lecture hall. A man is a man is a man.

There are two bad types that you should know about, because you'll be seeing some of each.

One is the hunter who knows everything *for sure*, and won't hesitate to tell you so, and who bitterly resents "college boy wildlifers." His stock in trade is some gray hair, several decades of seniority, and a big mouth. If you ever advised such a guy about *his* profession, he'd scream like a snowblind beaver trapper. All you can do is to give him courtesy and professional competence, although the odds are that he'll accept neither. But there is not much else you can do, for you are a pro.

Even worse, if possible, is the arrogant biologist. On the strength of a couple of college degrees, he scorns the hard-won experience of laymen. Overbearing and arrogant, scornful of the ideas of sportsmen, he does a bitter disservice to his profession. Go as far as you can in school, Johnny, but wear your academic degrees lightly. Give professional opinion when it is asked for, but give it in simple, direct terms. Save the professional jargon for the technical monographs. If a layman values your opinion enough to ask for it, don't make him feel the fool because he can't understand your answer. No man (and especially a real sportsman) will forgive another who makes a fool of him, or who ridicules his hard-won knowledge.

There'll also be anti-hunters who call you a paid butcher-boy working for gunners and interested only in killable animals. They will scorn and mock everything you stand for. Well, you'll never change them, so to hell with 'em!

Don't confuse such enemies with the many non-hunters who honestly want to help wildlife conservation but don't know how. They don't want to buy hunting licenses (and why should they?), yet they have no good, non-game wildlife conservation programs of their own. I hope this is changed by the time you go to work. Wildlife badly needs the support of the entire public— not just game species, but all kinds of wildlife. It's unfair to both the hunter and non-hunter to have the hunter supporting the wildlife conservation effort by himself.

Modern wildlife biology is a young profession. You will be only the *second* generation of specialized wildlife biologists. There's nothing else like it in the world. Our amazing North American wildlife populations, harvested by the millions year after year, don't just happen. They are maintained in a biological balance by a system of management that's driven by knowledge and dedication—and by people like you and your dad.

As a game biologist, you'll have one major job: to break down the barrier of mystery and misunderstanding between modern men and wildlife. You find the facts. How those facts are put to work is up to the nuts-and-bolts boys (the game managers) and the poor devil on the political firing line (your director). Your job is to get out there into the boonies and bring them back the best information you can get.

Maybe you're wondering: "Why put all that time and money and sweat into wildlife biology, when I could put it into something that pays better?"

Depends on what's meant by "pays better."

You'll never get rich as a wildlifer, and that's sure the truth. But a man is paid for his work in many ways, and money may be the least of these. Over the years I've had many successful men—engineers, businessmen, scientists, and even a few doctors—wistfully tell me that they wished they'd gone into wildlife work, which was where their hearts have really been all along.

I've been a wildlifer for nearly thirty years now, and I don't regret a minute of it. And it isn't just the fine places that you work in, or even the excitement of learning the secrets of fish and wildlife. A big part of it is the men you work with. You'll never meet a more colorful, loyal, dedicated team than the hard core of professional wildlifers. Sure, some of them are a little bush-happy, and inclined to shake hands with the willows, but they're mighty good men to float your stick with.

Looking back over my years of wildlife work, there are only two things that I'm plumb sure of: it's not easy work to prepare for or get into, but it's worth it. If I were your age, and knew everything that I know now, I'd do it all over again. And that, I reckon, is about the most that a man can say about his work.

If you want to take this up in more detail, I'd be happy to. But let's do it on a gravel bar on the Eleven Point River some fine evening while the first whipporwills are turning up and your dad washes the supper dishes.

Your friend,
John Madson

Poor Cousins

IN THE FAMILY OF AMERICAN WILDLIFE, the game animal is the rich uncle. It is studied, managed, and greatly valued by professional conservationists and sportsmen. Millions are spent each year on the management and hunting of deer, waterfowl, pheasants, quail, rabbits, and other game species.

Now consider their poor relatives: the nongame wildlife species.

They are no less beautiful or unique than the game species, nor less worthy of our concern. But because they are not hunted, they are not the subjects of intense, hunter-sponsored conservation programs. As Dr. Joe Linduska once wrote:

It is said that the bluebird is declining in numbers and is in trouble. That is a sad state of affairs, but it would probably not be so if the bluebird weighed three pounds and held well to a pointing dog . . .

If that bluebird, or any other nongame wildlife, is in trouble, it's not for lack of protection. Nearly all songbirds are protected by state and federal law. But while a bird may be protected from

185

shooting, it's not shielded from our technology. And to many wildlife species, the bulldozer, dragline and intensive farming are deadlier than bullets.

Protection is needed, of course. Even heavily hunted wildlife is protected—by closed seasons, bag limits, shooting hours, prescribed methods of take, and refuge areas. But protection alone won't do the job. By itself, it is generally a hands-off, do-nothing approach. The best protection for any wildlife species is positive management.

This has been proven with our major game species. We have learned a great deal about their biology, what makes them fail or flourish, and how to manage them as well as possible. There are gifted wildlife biologists who spend their entire careers studying a single game species and its environment.

Compared to pheasants and quail, we know practically nothing about orioles and bluebirds. And we debase ourselves and our world by saying: "So what? Bluebirds and orioles have no economic value . . . "

To anyone who loves nature in its completeness, it would be a dreary world with no wildlife but game species—no eagles, ospreys or hawks; no gulls or pelicans; no bobolinks, warblers, prairie dogs, kit foxes, coyotes, grebes, bitterns or flying squirrels, to say nothing of such desperately rare creatures as the lordly whooping crane, California crane, and peregrine falcon. And today, with man's heavy hand felt through all nature, it's time that we gave such creatures some of the priority attention that has been largely reserved for game animals and birds. We must broaden wildlife conservation to include all species of wildlife—not just the favored few.

Most Americans will never hunt, nor visit our great game ranges and see our most spectacular wildlife species. But that doesn't mean that they must be denied a chance to share America's wildlife splendor. The chance to enjoy quality wildlife in quality natural surroundings is an American birthright and a considerable part of the American dream.

Conservation of nongame wildlife has special meaning because it is everyday wildlife. It includes species that are adaptable to cities and suburbs if given half a chance: many songbirds, small hawks and owls, and such small game species as quail, cottontail rabbits and tree squirrels. All are animals that can be enjoyed in the back yard, at the bird-feeder, or in local parks and public gardens.

Another thing: if there's one lesson learned from a half-century of game management, it's that quality wildlife is the truest indicator of quality natural environment. You won't see an oriole or an indigo bunting in the slums of the Inner City; such habitat is occupied by house sparrows, rats and starlings. Orioles and buntings are fussy about environment. They are originals, and they demand something of original quality where they live. And as they are biological indicators of quality in their world, so they also indicate quality in ours. If there are fewer songbirds in our suburbs today, it's because the environment for birds has been degraded there—as well as the environment for children.

If we need more "practical" reasons than those for conserving nongame wildlife, there are some:

There was a time when all our domestic animals and plants were wild stock. Certain wild grasses became corn, rice and sugar cane. Bison were bred to become cattle; junglefowl to be Leghorn hens; wolves into man's best friend. All of man's domestic foods and animals had wild beginnings, and were once parts of original environment.

No man can say that today's "unused" wildlife may not have incalculable value in times ahead. Not long ago, it was found that something in the blood of abalones is tremendously effective against certain staphylococcus bacteria of the types that are building immunity to our best antibiotics. Recently, a rare desert plant in the Southwest was found to contain a strange wax with an extremely high melting point, useful in hardening certain lubes for heavy machinery. Until 1929, *Penicillium* mold was simply crud that formed on spoiled bread—and it has since become one of man's supreme blessings. The guinea pig has been a crucial ally in our war against disease, and the fruit fly *Drosophila* has taught us things about genetics that echo through our daily lives.

Every living thing on earth is unique. Once gone, it can never be replaced. It is part of what scientists call our "genetic pool"—the great reservoir of life on earth. Evolution, and unknown combinations and mutations of genes within that reservoir will certainly produce forms of life in ages to come that we cannot know about today. As passengers on this spaceship Earth, we'd be foolish to wipe out any of our shipmates. They will at least make our voyage less lonely as we drift through the endless, lifeless reaches of space—and they probably will make us wiser and better, as well. Many years ago, a naturalist named William Beebe wrote:

The beauty and genius of a work of art may be reconceived, harmony may yet again inspire the composer, but when the last individual of a race of living things breathes no more, another heaven and another earth must pass before such a one can be again.

Millions of Americans know this, and long to be part of a movement to prevent it. But they have always lacked ways and means to do so. They do not wish to buy hunting and fishing licenses that they will never use, and why should they? Besides, their main interest may be in nongame wildlife, not game species. Yet, there is no way for the average, non-hunting citizen to engage in general wildlife conservation programs.

This has concerned game managers and biologists for a long time—and that concern has begun to jell into workable, practical programs for expanding a state's game management efforts into nongame wildlife conservation.

The adoption of such programs could have repercussions all through the citizen environment—not only giving the average man a real piece of the conservation action, but providing a launching pad for a whole new system of environmental involvement.

No one method of funding this nongame wildlife and endangered species effort will fit all states. However, it is widely agreed that funding must come from sources other than fish and game funds. Historically, this concept was part of the American Game Policy of 1930, a landmark in American conservation that recognized the nonshooting protectionist and the scientist "as sharing with the sportsman and landowner the responsibility for wildlife conservation, with public funds from general taxation to better wildlife as a whole and the sportsman paying for all betterments serving game alone."

In what ways can those "public funds" be provided? Among the possibilities:

1. The state legislature to allocate, from the general fund, an appropriation related to a set percentage of the annual collection of fish and game funds.

Such an allocation would emphasize the need for cooperation in wildlife conservation and help unite the hunting and non-hunting publics in a common venture.

2. An annual appropriation for the general fund provided by a small per capita tax based on the number of residents within the state.

Such an appropriation would escalate with the population increase and provide more monies as fish and game resources face the mounting pressures of a rising human population. As such population rises, so does the need for intensive management of all wildlife species. This appropriation would not be measured as a percentage of fishing and hunting license revenue—which may be expected to decrease with large increases in population.

3. Earmarked Taxes

Although such taxes are anathema to many legislators, such a system has been in effect for many years and has provided fish and wildlife with hundreds of millions of dollars through special excise taxes on fishing tackle and sporting arms and ammunition. A similar system of excise taxes on cameras, film, binoculars, camping equipment, etc. has been proposed for the support of nongame wildlife programs.

Missouri, always in the vanguard of conservation progress, recently approved a state constitutional amendment that would earmark a fraction of the state's retail sales tax for conservation.

It is expected to provide an additional $21 million annually, much of which will finance new efforts in nongame management.

4. Grants, gifts and bequests from private sources.

This type of funding should be encouraged, and ways and means found to make it tax-deductible.

Once passed, new acts for nongame wildlife can quickly be put into gear. The basic, highly refined techniques of game management can be effectively applied to the problems of nongame wildlife conservation. Manning the program with premium talent is no problem: there is a corps of trained wildlife managers and biologists available—young, concerned, and desperately eager to help put such programs into action.

So all the elements for effective action exist: a critical public need, the techniques, knowledge, and trained men and women to meet that need, and equitable ways to provide the necessary funding.

The Dragons
Are Bigger Today

MORE TIMES THAN WE CAN REMEMBER, we've been asked about hunting in the future. As game managers, our reply must weigh two basic variables: the amount of huntable game that the land produces, and the amount of huntable land producing that game. Both of these factors, of course, depend upon a master variable: future land use. We know that maximum crop production is incompatible with maximum production of wildlife. The big question is whether land in the future will be in *maximum* production, or in *optimum* production—and the two are not necessarily the same.

Dr. Charles Hitch, President of Resources for the Future, Inc., has said that the United States can feed 300 million Americans at current levels of consumption and still be a major agricultural exporter.

Other authorities in the field of land use economics agree that our land and water supplies are sufficiently large and productive to meet our domestic demands and allow some of those basic resources to be used for recreation, wildlife, and other non-food

191

and fiber uses until at least the year 2000. These authorities believe that if there is no great increase in export demand, nor a stringent tightening of environmental controls in agriculture, there will be a surplus production capacity in the year 2000 and a large amount of land can be idled under government supply programs and diverted to other uses. Since political pressures generally require that such idled land be distributed proportionately across the nation—and largely devoted to grasses and forage crops—this could mean a favorable future for widespread, nationally distributed wildlife production. In terms of small game production in particular, dramatic results could occur almost overnight.

However, this implies "no great increase in export demand." What would result from a serious long-term effort to feed all developing nations, or to balance unlimited petrodollars with unlimited corn and wheat dollars? What would it cost in terms of basic soil and wildlife productivity?

If our future land use is generally scaled to our needs and reasonable export levels, we would be in a better position to conserve our land base and the quality environments that embellish it. But in terms of foreign policy and balance of trade, will such optimum land use be permissible? Developing nations are beginning to demand that the affluent nations share their wealth, and our own lop-sided level of consumption is beginning to concern some Americans. In the Lou Harris poll of December 1, 1975, it was noted that a 61-23 percent majority of the American people felt that it is "morally wrong" for us to consume 40 percent of the world's production of energy and raw materials—and a 50-31 percent plurality is worried that a continuation of this level of consumption of the world's resources "will turn the rest of the people of the world against us."

Philosophically, we may be caught between a rock and a hard place. Considering world need, how can we justify the allocation of any land resources to wildlife—and to recreational uses of wildlife that may keep land out of full production? How can we justify the existence of such marshes that could be producing wheat for export? The margin of productivity that is now sustaining wildlife is one of the resource margins needed by nations whose populations are outstripping their food production. In good conscience, can we put ducks above people?

Yet, many of us believe that wildlife is an infallible indicator of quality natural environments—and that freedom in such environments is the essence of the American Dream. If we were to engage in all-out maximum crop production in a serious effort to more evenly distribute the world's resource consumption, we might not only be exporting our basic land productivity and the wildlife that reflects it, but we might be losing a significant part of the American Dream—a part that is a highly perishable commodity that could never survive export. Yet, it would be even more foolish to maximize land use for domestic consumption alone—lowering our quality of life while we escalate our standard of living. The definition of our future happiness may be the precise definition of resource conservation.

The quality of wildlife in the future will depend largely upon the variables of land-use policy and economics. However, the quality of hunting that wildlife will depend largely on one constant: the hunter himself.

Whatever the future holds for hunting, good or bad, the hunter has probably got coming to him. If game management continues to enhance and regulate the game supply, it will be due to the financial, moral and political support of the hunter. If game management is corroded and weakened by political spoilers, it will be largely due to the inaction and indifference of the hunter—and his hunting will lose by default. Game management depends on the hunter, and the quality of hunting will be determined by the quality of the hunter, today and tomorrow. Whatever friends and allies he has, he'll have earned. And whatever enemies the hunter has, he'll probably have earned also.

A number of surveys have indicated that much of the so-called "anti-hunting sentiment" is essentially anti-hunter sentiment. There's a difference. Many of our critics are not opposed to the hunting of wildlife so much as the ways in which wildlife is hunted. They are not really against hunting in principle, but hunting in practice. There are, of course, zealots who are unalterably opposed to hunting in any form, for any reason, but we're inclined to believe that they are in the great minority. There's not much point in dwelling on them, for they are utterly blind to any position but their own and they will never join us on common ground from which we can fight common enemies.

If there is good hunting in the future it will be because the average hunter has shown a greatly increased willingness to cause and support such hunting; in other words, a man who has largely abandoned the old myth of "free hunting" and has become willing to spend a great deal more in terms of some kind of coin: money, time, effort, or all three.

The greatest danger to hunting today is the chiseler who wants something for nothing. At no real expense of time *or* effort *or* money, he demands something to hunt and places to hunt it. He invests little knowledge in his act of hunting, and little sympathy or understanding of wildlife and its land base. He simply demands something for nothing—and the genuine hunter ends up paying for it.

If there's such a thing as good free hunting, I've never seen much of it. The good hunting I've had has averaged out costing a lot of time and effort—and some money, although I've usually had more time and sweat to spend than cash. Granted, the greatest benefit of good hunting is quality freedom in quality country. But in this lies the germ of hunting's own destruction, for too many hunters demand freedom afield, without concurrent willingness to pay the costs of freedom, and that can be the ruin of genuine hunting as we know it.

Now, a hunter may say, and understandably so, "Daily life has restrictions enough; I go hunting to find freedom and escape restrictions." However, this is impossible. The ethical hunter imposes special restrictions on himself when he goes afield, and a sure definition of the slob hunter is one who refuses to observe any restrictions in the course of his hunting, or accept any responsibility for his actions. This is an especially critical problem in hunting because, as Aldo Leopold pointed out, "The hunter ordinarily has no gallery to applaud or disapprove his

conduct. Whatever his acts, they are dictated by his own conscience, rather than by a mob of onlookers."

I know a guide down in Stuttgart who is highly offended by
the term "arkansawing" ducks. He's plumb opposed to shooting
ducks on the water, and once told me: "A man who does a thing
like that ain't got no heart—all he's got is a thumpin' gizzard."

And there's the problem: how do you prevent a heart from
becoming a thumpin' gizzard?

We can't think of a more immediate way than effective hunter safety training programs. Some states now have good programs in force and are working to expand and improve them,
but other states are still doddering along with weak hunter
safety programs or none at all. We believe that these should be
mandatory, high-budget, top-priority programs with stringent
requirements, competent instructors, and first-class teaching
materials. The programs must involve gun safety, of course. But
just as important, they must entail basic instruction in conservation, hunting ethics and practices, and instill an abiding intoler-
ance for slob hunters.

Ten years ago we were lukewarm about hunter safety training. But now we're convinced that good hunter training is· a
practical and effective approach, and we're doing our best to
promote it. There are other practical approaches, too. Stiffer
trespass laws, for example. We feel that unauthorized trespass
by hunters should not be just listed in the game and fish code, or
in the civil code, but should be an offense included in the
criminal code and enforceable by all peace officers. It should
entail maximum penalties. Which sounds pretty strong, but
remember: the commonest offense of the slob hunter is unauthorized trespass, and the commonest form of anti-hunter is the
outraged landowner whose property rights have been violated.

And always, underlying everything else, there must be effective, professional management. Its main product may always be
huntable game, for that is the commodity that attracts the
investors. But it goes beyond that, for it is a process that can
help instill a land ethic in a landless public by providing a whole
range of human experiences with wildlife in quality natural

environments. Professional game management can produce more wildlife for everyone. And in doing so, it may produce something far more important: a growing state of harmony between men and land. Such management is the only solid ground from which we can defend the sport of hunting—and the lack of it is the only solid ground from which our enemies can attack.

There's an interesting line in the movie *Three Days of the Condor*. An old spy is talking to a young spy. The kid has heard that the senior spy dates back to the OSS and World War II, and the old-timer replies: "Yes, and even before that. And I certainly miss those days." "Oh? What do you miss—all the action that you had then?" "No," is the reply, "I miss the clarity."

Many of us miss the clarity with which we viewed game management twenty-five years ago, when we were younger and the dragons were smaller. But however the problems have grown, so has the new breed of men and women who'll be facing them. Next week, my son Chris will take his orals for the M.S. degree in wildlife ecology at the University of Wisconsin. In his peer group he is nothing unusual—but he's far smarter, better trained, and better equipped than his father. He has to be, for his dragons are bigger.

His allies, the genuine hunters, face those same dragons. They, too, will have to be better trained than their forebears. If there is good hunting in the future, it will be caused and practiced by people willing to pay their dues in terms of time, money, and effort, and who proudly accept the restrictions that ethical field conduct imposes. These are not just the requirements of an increasingly critical society, but also of increasingly vulnerable environments. The same qualities that will help make the hunter acceptable to society as a whole will also impel him to fight for the quality landscapes that produce and support game surpluses. His deepening commitment will not only provide a solid ethical base for his act of hunting, but a solid political base from which he can help perpetuate quality country and its wildlife component.

Again, we're not saying that this ideal *will* develop, but that it *must* develop. Through almost all of human existence, huntable land and huntable wildlife have preceded the hunter. They *caused* the hunter. But in the future this must be reversed. It is the hunter who must cause huntable land and wildlife, and a world worth being young in.

Something
for the Kids

THIS HAPPENED OUT THERE IN THE HIGH COUNTRY, which is about the only place it would happen, old field men being what they are.

There are things that those jaspers just don't talk about much, partly because they can never say it the way they feel it, and partly because the men they'd say it to already know, anyway. But now and then, out somewhere back of beyond or over in the high lonesome, a seasoned ranger or game warden will start jawing and reveal something of the dreams and hopes that impel him.

Five of us were ending a long day around the evening fire just under timberline. We were on our way out of the summer elk range and were camped on a timbered bench above a creek that flashed with cutthroat trout, a diamond of a place, with the night wind carrying the rumble of sliding talus from the other side of the valley. We had topped out at noon, coming over the Divide in a sleet storm and drifting down toward treeline behind a band of elk. We were two days' ride from the nearest fence

199

and now, full of trout and sourdough biscuits, we loafed beside the bull fire and talked it over.

We had been working most of the week in the high elk range—a game warden, a forest ranger, a biologist, a writer, and the supervisor. Total conservation mileage: about 150 years. And for some reason the talk turned away from horses, hunting, and women, and got to be a seminar on conservation. It didn't last long. The men around that fire weren't given to much high-blown philosophy. But this is the way it went:

They spoke of wild country that has become the battle ground of the spoilers and savers. The spoilers being self-serving politicians, the dam builders, poachers, certain stockmen and miners and lumbermen, but mostly just people who don't give a damn. The savers were men trying to co-exist with the mountains. Men with one foot in yesterday and the other in tomorrow, standing foursquare for the great places. It was the solemn opinion of this whiskery campfire congress that the savers might not be very smart, and would likely die as broke as the Ten Commandments, but that they'd never feel any shame when they looked back at the country they'd come through.

The ranger, a grizzled man grown old in the Forest Service, leaned back against a pannier and spat an amber stream of tobacco juice at a coal beside the fire. He eyed the sizzling result with satisfaction and said: "By God, let's see Smokey the Bear do *that!*" He paused, and went on:

"I've seen some bad fires and some spoilers that were about as bad, and I've fought both. Been roasted by fires and politicians, but I'll probably fight some more before my string runs out. Partly because it's my job, but mostly because these mountains are the only thing I got.

"Sure, I got a place and a good wife, and a pack of grandkids that I think the world of, but all that is part of mind and memory, sort of, and everything but the love I have for them is bound to fade and go. But these mountains are always here.

"First time I rode over that divide where we crossed today, I wasn't old enough to vote. I was full of juice, let me tell you! I could peg an axe ten hours a day and still have enough pepper to go courting or fight rough-and-tumble. I've changed some, since then, but the mountains haven't. Plenty changes farther down, with all the roads and more people all the time. But change comes slower up here.

"I got a grandson who's sixteen years old. That means that I may see the day when my great-grandson comes riding over that same ridge up there, full of pepper just like I was. Think of that! I hope he sees the same things I seen, the same old mountains and snowfields and timber and all, and feels the same things I felt.

"These days I think a lot about all the grandsons, and their kids, and the things they got a right to. And if they never get a chance to see this country the way it ought to be, the way a free-born man or woman's got a right to see it, and if there ain't no more wild divides to top out over, or tall timber to camp by, I reckon it would bust my heart."

The backlog caught, lighting the circle of faces. A freshening breeze came down from the high snow, pressing us closer to the fire, and a horse bell pealed in the pasture below.

Jinglebob, the old game warden, stood and turned his backside to the fire.

Like the ranger, he had grown old in public service. Everything about him bespoke experience and hard wear. His legs, sheathed in shotgun chaps cut from the hide of a record elk, were bowed from forty years of saddle. He was a spare man, narrow-waisted and buttless like many old riders are, and even in his runover boots he stood less than six feet tall.

"Tall timber, tall timber," he said mournfully. "Pete, that's all we hear from you. When you cash in, I reckon we'll just plant you in a reforestation project and mulch you down good and see if you'll grow. You old woodpeckers are all alike.

"But I suppose I know what you mean. Take them elk we seen today. No such thing when I was a kid. This country had been throwed and rolled on. Game was about done for. What little the market hunters, miners, and outlaw Utes had left, the shirt-tail ranchers tried to finish off. But we've worked damn hard, and we've got something again.

"I like to ride the high country as well as the next man. But a mountain ain't much but high rock and snow and calendar pictures if it ain't got something alive on it. Sure, a good mountain has got to have good timber. But the mountain ought to have a few good rams, maybe, and some elk, and a couple lions and bears to give 'em exercise. And some good high lakes with native trout in 'em, and good cricks down below where a hungry pilgrim can take a mess of fish. Without that, a mountain just ain't alive.

"Lot of times, I've been out on patrol and run plumb out of groceries, maybe, and spent the last few days eating bannock and beavertail. I'd get home tired and sore, with my outfit about wore out and the wife worried and mad, and I'd wonder why in hell I wasn't back on the Turkeyfoot again, raising beef and sleeping in a bed.

"Then next day I'd meet some little kid in town and he'd say: 'Mr. Jo-Bob, what did you see this time? You see any grizzlies or lions up there? You ketch any big fish? Kin you take me along, sometime?'

"And then I'd tell him about some high claw sign on a tree up on the Sunlight, or a bull elk that would go sixteen hands at the withers, or about the awful big trout I'd of landed if I hadn't got careless.

"And in no time at all, there'd be three or four more kids around, listening, and pretty soon a couple of men would drift over, and their eyes would light up just like the kids' would.

"I don't reckon there's such a thing as a *grown* man. Not where wild critters are concerned. When it comes to fish and game, all men are just kids. Well, I never arrest a bad violator without thinking of what he's trying to take away. He's trying to rub the clawmarks off that tree up on Sunlight, or steal a kid's first big trout, or take the last royal bull off the mountain.

"Then what does a man say when he's stopped on the street some day by a kid who asks: 'Mister, did you see my trout? Is

there an elk up there for me, when I'm grown enough to hunt?'
And the man has to say: 'I'm sorry, boy. There ain't no elk left
for you. No trout, either. All used up, and poisoned, and gone.'

"Maybe I ain't much of a warden, but I sure try. And what I
try for is this: that fifty or a hundred years from now, some
shiny eyed kid can run up to some man and say: 'Mister, what
did you see in the high country this time out? Are the big elk
still there?' And the man can grin and say: 'They sure are, son—
there and waitin' for you!'"

We slept on that and we slept well, as men in the mountains
do. In the deep shadows of the valley floor the little cutthroat
creek shouted off through the night on its ageless journey to the
Vallecito. Above and around us stood the eternal, encircling
ranges, awaiting the hundred generations.

Credits

"Message from a Desert Island" From *Audubon*, January, 1974. Reprinted by permission.

"Requiem for a Small River" From "A Plague on All Your Rivers," *Audubon*, September, 1972. Reprinted by permission.

"The Running Country" From *Audubon*, July, 1972. Reprinted by permission.

"The Prairie Blizzard" From *Audubon*, March, 1970. Reprinted by permission.

"Where the River Fits the Song" From *Audubon*, September, 1974. Reprinted by permission.

"The High Beyond" From "The Elk," Conservation Department of Winchester-Western, Olin Corporation, 1966. Reprinted by permission.

"Giants in the Cliffs" From *Audubon*, November, 1976. Reprinted by permission.

"The Dance on Monkey Mountain" From *Audubon,* January, 1976. Reprinted by permission.

"Day of the Crane" From *Audubon*, March, 1974. Reprinted by permission.

"North Again" From *Audubon*, March, 1977. Reprinted by permission.

"A Letter to a Young Trapper" From *Guns* & *Ammo*, September, 1972. Reprinted by permission.

"Poor Cousins" From "A Law for Wildlife," Conservation Department of Winchester-Western, Olin Corporation, 1972. Reprinted by permission.

"The Dragons Are Bigger Today" Address to the 22nd Annual Conservation Conference of the National Wildlife Federation, December 10, 1975.